"In *A Hill of Beans: The Grace of Everyday Troubles*, Valerie Schultz offers a rich feast of hard-earned insights born from an honest, searching life of faith. Along the way, she invites readers to discover how God's grace is found both within and beyond the sacramental life of the Church: in the joys and struggles of ever-changing family dynamics, in lean times of recession and career detours, in empty nesting and church disaffiliation, in caring for a loved one with addiction, and even in experiences of tragic suffering."

—Michael J. Sanem, a former Bernardin Scholar at Catholic Theological Union, ministers in Kansas City, where he lives with his wife and three sons. He is author of the recently released *Your Church Wants to Hear from You: What Is the Synod on Synodality?* and writes regularly at *incarnationiseverywhere.com.*

"Valerie Schultz wants us to know that praying for the small things is not silly but sacred. With humility and humor, she reminds us that God's love and mercy surround us at every moment, whether we are coping with an ancient dog or facing the searing devastation of a child's addiction. In sharing her struggle to get through a year of teaching, Schultz teaches us to see our failures as journeys and to have the eyes to recognize each other as companions along the way. Through the veil of her own pains and joys, Schultz encourages us to hold up a mirror to our own lives and see where we might ask God for grace and mercy."

—Michelle Francl-Donnay is a wife and mother, a professor of chemistry, and an adjunct scholar at the Vatican Observatory. She is author of *Prayer: Biblical Wisdom for Seeking God* in the *Little Rock Scripture Study Alive in the Word* series. Her website is *michellefrancldonnay.com.*

D1490610

A Hill of Beans

The Grace of Everyday Troubles

Valerie Schultz

A *Give Us This Day* Book

LITURGICAL PRESS
Collegeville, Minnesota

www.litpress.org

2	3	4	5	6	7	8	9

Library of Congress Cataloging-in-Publication Data

Names: Schultz, Valerie, author.
Title: A hill of beans : the grace of everyday troubles / Valerie Schultz.
Description: Collegeville, Minnesota : Liturgical Press, [2022] | "A Give Us This Day Book."
Identifiers: LCCN 2022014807 (print) | LCCN 2022014808 (ebook) | ISBN 9780814667798 (paperback) | ISBN 9780814667804 (epub) | ISBN 9780814667804 (pdf)
Subjects: LCSH: Schultz, Valerie. | Christian biography. | Christian life. | BISAC: RELIGION / Christian Living / Inspirational | RELIGION / Spirituality
Classification: LCC BR1725.S384 (ebook) | LCC BR1725.S384 A3 2022 (print) | DDC 270.092 [B 23›eng›20220] —dc21
LC record available at https://lccn.loc.gov/2022014807
LC ebook record available at https://lccn.loc.gov/2022014808

Dedicated to Randy, my soul mate,
my best mate, my far better half

Contents

MORTALITY/DEATH

"Jesus does not want to come merely in the little things of our lives, but also *in our own littleness*: in our experience of feeling weak, frail, inadequate, perhaps even 'messed-up.'"

—Pope Francis, Midnight Mass on Christmas, 2021

Introduction

You might feel it sometimes when you look up at a clear night sky, at the scads of faraway stars and the vastness of the universe: you sense your own smallness. It can happen when you lose someone you love, and you compare the short span of a human life to the millions of years of history. Or when you are stuck on a freeway and speculate about the identities and experiences of the hundreds of strangers whom you will likely never know, occupying the cars inching forward in the other lanes. You are conscious of the insignificance of the present instant in the context of all the past and future ones, and the irrelevance of one person, yourself included. It's a humbling moment, perhaps tinged with melancholy.

This blue feeling reminds me of the dramatic climax of one of my favorite movies, *Casablanca*, when Humphrey Bogart as Rick tells Ingrid Bergman as Ilsa that "the problems of three little people don't amount to a hill of beans in this crazy world."

Rick is right. Most of us are little people. Most of us do not have problems with any global consequence. But our problems can be enormous to us, and the way we solve or don't solve them can determine the course of our lives. It occurs to me that we do ourselves an injustice by minimizing the issues we face to hill-of-beans status.

Because as people of faith, we know that God cares about the problems of little people. God knows every last little bean. God walks with us through our quandaries and difficulties and doubts. We may feel silly bringing our everyday worries to God in prayer, but Jesus teaches us that in God's eyes, we amount to everything. "Are not five sparrows sold for two small coins?" Jesus asks. "Yet not one of them has escaped the notice of God. Even the hairs of your head have all been counted. Do not be afraid. You are worth more than many sparrows" (Luke 12:6-7). Setting aside the fact that sparrows are not on our shopping lists these days, we get the point.

The sacred texts often reassure us of how much we matter to God. Psalm 139, for example, reminds us that God sees us as we are: "My very self you know. / My bones are not hidden from you" (Ps 139:14-15). We begin to understand that each seemingly slight hill of beans in our lives is known and dear to God, because of God's unbounded love for us. The psalm makes our relationship to God personal: "Probe me, God, know my heart; / try me, know my thoughts. / See if there is a wicked path in me; / lead me along an ancient path" (Ps 139:23-24). The low altitude of our particular hill of beans matters not to our all-caring God, who will lead us if we ask.

Circling back to the lessons of *Casablanca . . . .* My husband and I are such fans that we danced our first married dance to "As Time Goes By." The song Sam plays under duress is our song. Yet when our youngest daughter finally acquiesced to watching this beloved old black-and-white movie with her parents, the ending horrified her. "Why do you LIKE this movie?" she asked us, utterly dismayed that the characters, upon realizing that their problems don't amount to a hill of beans, do not get the happy ending they deserve, the one she expected. Even so, the greater good is served, a beautiful friendship begins, and surely God notices their selfless act.

Because God notices all of us, in our goodness and in our struggles and in our failures.

"What is man that you are mindful of him?" asks the psalmist (Ps 8:5). I can almost picture God with a twinkling eye, answering with Rick's toast for the ages: "Here's looking at you, kid."

Author's note on my long-suffering family: I remember a moment of uncomfortable recognition when my husband and I saw the movie *Something's Gotta Give*, in which Diane Keaton portrays a well-regarded playwright. Jack Nicholson's character, Harry, is discomfited to find, almost verbatim, scenes from their past relationship in her new play. He feels exposed and embarrassed. But it's not really him, the writer explains: the play's character is named Henry, not Harry. Besides, Henry is killed off in Act Two (which doesn't exactly set Harry's mind at ease). I believe my husband found much with which to identify in that scene of the film. As did I: writers will mine the gems of life without mercy.

In nonfiction, however, the real-life subjects have nowhere to hide. My children have grown up with a mother who speculates about them and parses them publicly, and while they may think this is normal, it is something about which I am periodically seized with guilt. A writer, as Joan Didion noted, is "always selling somebody out." I worry that I have shamelessly exploited our family experiences for the sake of a deadline. I worry that my loved ones appear in print more frequently than they might appreciate. But once, while visiting one of my kids in a college dorm, I was surprised and delighted to see a column I'd written posted on the door for all to read. So perhaps my darlings have not been scarred for life.

My husband and children are like the angels and saints in how they deal with having a wife and mother who uses them for raw material. They are gracious in the face of exposure, and have definitely suffered for the sake of art. They love me anyway.

My children, in their blooming lives, have given and continue to give me plenty to write about. They do things of which I do not approve. They make choices that make me look bad. They mystify me and madden me. But they also make me proud and make me laugh, make me mindful and make me grateful, make my heart stretch beyond its limits and make my soul soar. They've even made me a grandmother. I pray that they will always recognize the hand and the voice of God in their lives. May they reach for the stars and walk on firm ground. May they be their best selves.

(*And one more thing, a note on dates:* Rather than organizing these essays chronologically, I've presented them by theme. To help dispel any timeline confusion, I've followed each title by the year in which it was written.)

Not Belonging/Alienation

The Message in the Machine

(2012)

My husband finally got me to see the movie *Hugo*. I'd had no desire to see it when it was first out in the theaters, because it had been advertised as a 3D film. In my biased mind, 3D means all show, no substance. Plus I don't want to have to wear cheesy glasses over my actual glasses for two hours. Plus the things rushing at me in 3D productions make me feel a little nauseous. I know: I'm old.

My husband really wanted to see *Hugo*, but I kept deflecting him. We finally saw it last week, sans glasses, and I've been thinking about it ever since. The joke was on me, because I adored this movie, possibly more than my husband did. I now recommend it to everyone. *Hugo* is masterful. It is visually lovely, well-written, beautifully acted, and directed by a pro (Scorsese!). It is sweet, funny, heartbreaking, suspenseful, educational, and the bearer of a fantastic message.

The movie *Hugo* is based on a book called *The Invention of Hugo Cabret*. The author, Brian Selznick, wrote and illustrated such a beguiling hybrid of a novel and a storybook that he won the 2008 Caldecott Medal, which is normally given to a traditional picture book. The plot centers on an orphan's tale. When Hugo's father dies, Hugo is taken in by a drunken uncle who makes his living by winding all the clocks in a busy train station in 1930s Paris. When the uncle disappears, Hugo continues to wind the clocks so that no one notices his uncle's absence. He lives alone in the walls of the station, steals food, hides on the margins, and breaks the viewer's heart. Hugo has inherited his father's love and talent for machines. With patience beyond his years, Hugo tinkers with and fixes all kinds of mechanisms. His true goal is to resurrect the strange, sad-faced automaton—a mysterious mechanical man—that he and his father had been working on together. Hugo meets Isabelle, a comparably lonely girl who loves to read, but who craves actual adventure. The rest of the movie depicts Hugo and Isabelle's adventure together, intertwined with the origin of Hugo's automaton and the history of the motion picture, but I will stop short of spoilers: I don't want to ruin it for anyone.

But see it! It's the message of *Hugo* that has stayed with me. Isabelle has also lost her parents, although she lives with her godparents. Hugo explains to her, in an attempt to assuage her sense of loss, that he has found comfort in the depths of his grief by imagining the entire world as a machine. Machines, Hugo says, only come with exactly the parts they need, and nothing more. "So I figured," he tells her, "if the entire world was one big machine, I couldn't be an extra part. I had to be here for some reason. And that means you have to be here for some reason, too."

It struck me as deeply spiritual, this young boy's attempt to make sense of a seemingly nonsensical existence. I like thinking of the world as God's machine, as a wondrous invention in which every part is needed. We are metaphysical cogs, souls with different abilities and attributes and functions, but somehow we all fit together. And we are all necessary for the grand machine to work exactly as it's supposed to work.

Isabelle's godfather is an older gentleman who exemplifies one of the pitfalls of aging, in that he no longer feels he is a useful part of society. Many older people, especially upon retirement, feel worthless, alienated, cast off by the lives they used to lead. My mother often spoke of feeling "like a leftover" after my dad died. It was like she'd lost sight of her proper place in the world, and instead saw a future in which she was an ill fit, an extra. Hugo tells Isabelle that it makes him sad when a machine is broken, because it can't perform its function. "Maybe it's the same with people," he says. "If you lose your purpose, it's like you're broken."

Hugo and Isabelle eventually offer an avenue of redemption for her godfather's brokenness, which is another reason to love this movie. Like Hugo, I don't believe we ever become spare parts. We are not created for despair. Our purpose may change, but we remain essential to the whole. Not one of us, in the divine scheme of things, is extra. We are needed. We belong.

If that's not a message from God, I don't know what is.

Daughter of Doubt

(2002)

I t had to happen. Just as the shoemaker's children go bare-foot and the carpenter's children live under a leaky roof, I knew this day would come. I am a church worker whose child has stopped going to church.

My children have grown up with the church as their second home, as it was pretty much accepted that if I were not at home, I was at the church. In my role as a director of religious education, I've had small students ask me if I lived in my office, or if I were a nun. My own children have an easy comfort both with the church itself and the accompanying facilities that has always warmed me. They have helped set up, run, and clean up a slew of activities over the years, and with very little grumbling. They've also had fun with friends at different ages and in various programs. The church has been good for all of us, and vice versa.

I expected this to happen when my oldest daughter left for college. After all, one of the first things I let slide in college was Sunday Mass, or even faking going to Sunday Mass, which I had perfected in my last year of high school. But my oldest found a Saturday evening Mass with music she liked and still attends regularly, even adding her hard-earned minimum-wage dollars to the collection. She has made me happy and proud to be such a good mother.

So what do I do with another daughter, a senior in high school who will leave home in the fall, who has been confirmed and co-teaches a kindergarten religious education class, and who faked sick three Sundays in a row until finally admitting that she just doesn't think she buys into this Catholic jazz? Scratch that bit about being a good mother.

My first reaction was the typical "As long as you're under my roof, you'll do what I say" approach. But interestingly enough, it was my husband, whom our children see as the stricter parent, who questioned the wisdom of force-feeding faith. It's not like she's a young child, he reasoned with me. She made the choice to be confirmed as a Catholic last year. Now the decision really is hers, if we practice what we say we believe.

And there it is. It is so much easier to preach things when they pertain to other people's children. How many parents I have counseled to let their young adult children find their own way, to be patient and hopeful, that as parents all they can do is model their faith by the way they live their lives: I should listen to myself! But this is my kid, and I find my heart is breaking.

When we finally talk, my daughter is angry. The rampant revelations of sexual abuse by priests have fueled her doubts; certainly the hypocrisy she perceives in supposed people of faith who conduct themselves as people of hate violates her sense of justice. I have no good answers for these indefensible human acts. I understand her doubt because I have been there. That, alas, she cannot see.

I wonder how many other people see me as she does: upright, strong, committed perhaps to a fault, faithful without doubt. It is my veneer. She doesn't see that I wrestle with some of the same issues she does. In fact, as much as my oldest may get her unquestioning Mass attendance from me, this daughter may get her discomfort with the zealous from me. I have seen her squirm at Youth Days in the face of boundless, hand-clapping, Hosanna-shouting energy, as well as when an acquaintance peppers her conversation with holy ejaculations ("It's a beautiful day, praise God! Praise God in Heaven!!"), and so do I. I just hide it well. She doesn't see it or believe that I could possibly understand.

And part of me doesn't understand. Life without the Eucharist seems a barren place to me, and I have to remember that her denial of the sacrament is not permanent. She assures me at the end of our conversation that she is not closing any doors. She believes something, even if she doesn't know quite what that is. She still wants to work at the soup kitchen, and I am relieved that her sense of social justice, always a bright light in her, seems undimmed.

Perhaps she will find God in other places. I hope that perhaps someday, a whiff of the smoky incense she once carried into church as a young dancer will remind her of where she truly belongs. Perhaps an Angelus bell ringing in a distant city, or the face of Christ at a soup kitchen, or her love for ritual and poetry will call her back. Perhaps a future crisis will provide her with her own pair of spiritual ruby slippers, which she'll click all the way to the altar as she realizes that there's no place like home. And that our Church is a place with ample room for flaws and doubt and darkness, as well as plenty of faith and light. For people with struggling minds and suffering, loving hearts, just like her.

For now, her empty place in the pew each Sunday is one of those sad thorns among the lovely roses of motherhood. Praise God.

My Burden Is Light

(2014)

This is usually how I operate: A dilemma arises, over which I worry and fret and make lists of pros & cons and lose sleep. I debate, I research, I agonize. Then, when I am at my wits' end, I remember to take a breath, and pray.

Why is prayer so often my last resort rather than my first? My life pattern is that at each crisis or turning point, I must relearn that I need divine help. Over the years, the following verses, drawn from the Gospel of Matthew, have helped me to remember to pray: "Come to me, all you who labor and are burdened, and I will give you rest. Take my yoke upon you and learn from me, for I am meek and humble of heart; and you will find rest for yourselves. For my yoke is easy, and my burden light" (Matt 11:28-30).

I love this Gospel reading. It reveals the tender side of Jesus, the Jesus who so obviously loves us, who comforts us and shoulders our baggage and sits with us when we most need a friend. This is the gentle Jesus, the "humble of heart." This is the Jesus I find in prayer, if I only take the time to pray. I recently came across a page in an old journal where I had copied these verses from Matthew, and later penciled below it, "Keep saying it, Jesus: I forget."

"Come to me," says Jesus, inviting us to lay down our worldly burdens and exchange them for a lighter one. Prayer is how we send an RSVP to his invitation. When we are world-weary, we long for the rest that comes from a spiritual embrace. No wonder we refer to a life-altering change of heart as a "Come-to-Jesus" moment. By responding to an invitation, we are transformed. When we do come to Jesus, the sense of completion is revelatory. The epiphany dawns, the light shines, and we finally find that rest because, as St. Augustine pointed out, our hearts are restless until they rest in him.

These words of Jesus seem simple, yet they are words of nuance and depth. Biblical readings can sound contradictory, and the preaching of Jesus is no exception. For all the gentle promise of his words, there are times when his yoke does not always seem easy, and his burden does not always seem light. Might not a yoke, after all—a wooden crosspiece that tethers a pair of animals to a cart or a plow—remind us of the wooden crosspiece that Jesus carried to his own execution? His yoke may be the crosses we must carry in our own lives. "Take my yoke upon you and learn from me," says Jesus. We know from experience that when we rely on Jesus to help us carry the crosses we encounter in our lives, they are indeed lighter than when we try to drag them along the path on our own. The burden of following Jesus, then, is a blessing of paradox.

Whenever I read this Gospel, I feel myself surrender. I have to think of the act of surrendering not as a weak or negative event, not as a loss in battle, but as an act of trust. When we come to Jesus, when we give ourselves over to God's will, when we accept that metaphorical yoke, we can find rest. I just wish that I could hold on to that elusive peace rather than find myself heavily burdened yet again by temporal cares and worries. It seems that answering Jesus' invitation to come to him must be a daily affair. If I am to learn from Jesus, every day must become a teachable moment, especially when I am such a dense student. When I am weary, when I am burdened, when there is nothing left to do but pray, when I finally take the yoke of Jesus upon me, this is the moment of conversion. What has been heavy becomes as light as breath, and I rest. I have come home.

Nevertheless, She Persisted

(2017)

Senate Majority Leader Mitch McConnell inadvertently started something. I imagine McConnell might wish he had chosen less quotable words to compel Senator Elizabeth Warren to stop talking during a confirmation hearing for Attorney General Jeff Sessions. "She was warned. She was given an explanation," said McConnell in his signature monotone. "Nevertheless, she persisted."

And that's how a catchphrase is born. Also a slogan, a meme, a tattoo, a chant, a protest sign, a rallying cry. Online sites hawk t-shirts, sweatshirts, jewelry, and bumper stickers. Thus sayeth McConnell: *Nevertheless, she persisted!* It's a phrase we women embrace, because persistence is what we do.

I am reminded of the time my daughter, when she was a teenager, used a biblical image to strengthen an argument. I can't remember what she wanted at the time—a later curfew or a raise in allowance—but she kept after me about it, bringing up the topic repeatedly. Finally she said, "I'm the persistent widow, Mom." And I realized she was alluding to the previous Sunday's Gospel reading. She had actually been listening to something in church! I was amazed and impressed. So naturally I rewarded her persistence, and her tactics.

The widow my daughter referred to appears in the Gospel of Luke. Jesus prefaces the parable with our need "to pray always without becoming weary" (Luke 18:1). The widow does not give up on asking for justice from a corrupt judge. She does what women must do: she persists. She wears the judge down until he gives in and rules in her favor, just to get rid of her. The powerless overcomes the powerful.

Stories of persistent women abound in the Gospels. There is the woman in the Gospel of Luke who suffers from excessive bleeding. She has endured much at the hands of many doctors, but she has not been cured. Society shuns her as unclean due to the ever-presence of menstrual blood. She persists in getting close enough to Jesus to touch the hem of his cloak, believing in Jesus' power to heal her. Her persistence and faith are rewarded (Luke 8:43-48).

There is the Canaanite woman in the Gospel of Matthew, a foreigner, who persists in believing that Jesus can help her daughter. Jesus answers that he was sent only to the Jews. "It is not right to take the food of the children and throw it to the dogs," he tells her (Matt 15:26). The disciples want Jesus to get rid of this pesky woman. But she persists: "Please, Lord, for even the dogs eat the scraps that fall from the table of their masters" (Matt 15:27). Because of her faith, Jesus heals her daughter. Her persistence validates Jesus' redemptive role for non-Jews.

There is the nameless woman in the Gospel of Luke, weeping and wordless, who washes Jesus' feet with her tears and dries them with her hair. She kisses his feet and anoints them with oil. She persists in caring for him, even when Jesus' dining companions condemn her as a sinner. Jesus forgives her sins, saying, "Your faith has saved you; go in peace" (Luke 7:50).

There are the women in the Gospel of John who persist in following Jesus all the way to the foot of the cross, when most of his other followers have abandoned him (John 19:25). Among them is Mary, the mother of Jesus, who loves her son with the persistent love we women hold for our children, and reflects the parental love that God has for us.

Throughout the Gospels, Jesus blesses the persistence of women when he equates it with faith, with prayer, with not losing heart. Atypically for his time, and in spite of the men around him who prefer that women stay quiet and go away, he listens to women. He converses with women. He acknowledges the worth of women. He understands that persistence is deeply tied to faith. Indeed, to this day, persistence in the cause of love and mercy requires a lot of faith and prayer and heart.

We women persist. Isn't that our job? Throughout history, we have persisted in our quest for respect, for justice, for equal rights, for suffrage, for education, for enfranchisement, for recognition, for making our voices heard. In the face of violence, of opposition, of ridicule, of belittlement, even of jail time, nevertheless, we have persisted.

And it's not over. It is perhaps never over. The many struggles of women continue around the world. We may suffer dissuasion, discouragement, and defeat. We will be warned and given explanations. Nevertheless, we persist.

Family Strife

What Makes a Family?

(2020)

The coronavirus pandemic has robbed many of us of the comfort of being with family. I'm speaking for myself. Although my oldest daughter and I talk weekly, we have seen each other in person only once since the sheltering-in-place got real in late March. She quarantined herself for fourteen days last month before visiting us, her parents whom she considers old enough to be at a high risk of infection. She lives alone, but she recently told me about spending time with a friend. "She's in my bubble," my daughter said, referring to the small group with whom she has been safely socializing in the time of COVID-19.

Lots of people are in similar bubbles now. The bubble is safe, but it has rules: you can only socialize within the bubble, you have to wear a mask, you have to observe the social distance of at least six feet, you should meet outside, and you have to leave the bubble if you've risked any exposure to the virus. In this way, while the pandemic has kept some families apart, it has also created intentional families.

I am reminded of the artificial extended families in Kurt Vonnegut's novel *Slapstick*, in which everyone is randomly assigned to a family of cousins with identifying middle names like Oriole-2 or Raspberry-19, so that everyone can feel they are "Lonesome No More!" In fact as in fiction, we sometimes establish families out of no-family when we have the need for family. Like now in our bubbles.

Families of people who are not genetically related are not new. From ancient times, religions have created families out of people who share a common creed rather than blood. The Gospel of Mark relates that when Jesus, surrounded by a crowd of listeners, was told that his mother and brothers were waiting outside to see him, "he said to them in reply, 'Who are my mother and brothers?' And looking around at those seated in the circle he said, 'Here are my mother and my brothers. Whoever does the will of God is my mother and brother and sister'" (Mark 3:33-35).

After Jesus was crucified, the family of Christian faith was born on Pentecost, when the Holy Spirit breathed on the frightened disciples huddled in the Upper Room. As these first evangelizers went out into the streets, the energy of faith fueled the fire within them. Not even different languages could separate this new family of believers (Acts 2:1-11; also John 20:19-23).

Blood families form the basic units of society, but we all know that they do not always stick together. A family can be pulled apart by misunderstandings, divorces, custody battles, inheritance lawsuits, betrayals, addictions, abuses, intolerance, prejudice, politics, and as many other reasons as there are possible disagreements. We have seen on our southern border that families can be separated against their will by law, by walls, by circumstances, or by the desire for a better life. A family can be a fragile construct indeed.

Relatives have even fallen out in these combative, polarizing times due to divergent COVID-19 practices. Those who mask will not meet with those who think masks infringe on their personal freedom. Those who observe social distance guide-lines will not accept invitations from those who do not. Hence the bubbles we draw around ourselves, as we become families of common practices and values. Blood may be thicker than water, but it isn't always enough to hold a family together.

"You aren't my grandma by blood," my step-grandson told me not long after my youngest daughter married his father, something I imagine he'd heard from grown-ups.

"True," I said. "I'm your grandma by love." That seemed an acceptable answer to my grandson. Blood families give us life, but open-hearted commitment is how family members support each other and grow together and even reach out to include others. The traditional family tree illustrates the branches of heredity, but the family ties that last are made of love. Maybe that's what our bubbles are made of. Maybe that's what Jesus meant.

Jaime and His Not-So-Sacred Life

(2005)

It's been a bad week.

Our dog Jaime, who is nearing fifteen, has tried my patience. In fact, he has killed my patience. He is deaf, nearsighted, arthritic, clueless, and severely flatulent. He has unsightly rubbery growths in his ears, a twisted spine, and terrible breath.

When he is in the house, we spend most of our time yelling at him to get out of the way. Worst of all, and there is no way to put this delicately, his sphincter no longer functions: the poop comes when it comes. No matter where he is. No matter who is visiting. The odor emanating from these accidents is paralyzing, stultifying, nostril-violating. On one recent morning, the smell in my bedroom woke me at 5:30. I put Jaime outside as I cleaned up his predawn deposit, which included a sepia stain on the carpet, as he had completely missed the old towel on which he sleeps. Since it was snowing, I slipped on my clogs before stepping outside to feed him. My first unthinking step outside, however, was smack into a steaming new nest of poop, which clung to and filled in the grooves of my shoe. My anger (expletives deleted) sent him scurrying into the neighbor's yard, whose fence is down because they are in the midst of replacing it with a do-it-yourself stone wall. By the time I cleaned off my shoe and called Jaime to come back home, he had managed to fall into the neighbor's pool. The day was still young, and my mood was already almost as foul as the wet-dog smell now mingling with the old-pooping-dog smell of which I was vainly trying to rid him.

On top of these many annoyances, my husband was out of town for a conference. While he was enjoying a private hotel room, catered meals, and intellectual stimulation, I was keeping the home fires burning. While he was presumably still asleep at 5:30 a.m., I was scrubbing the carpet and hauling the dog out of the neighbor's pool. And at the true root of my anger, *he* was the one who was adamant about not taking Jaime down the vet's green mile until he was beyond all hope. I was of the opinion that Jaime's life had been long and happy and was now plunging into pain and senility, and it was up to us to recognize that the inevitable was upon us.

As it happened, a friend of my daughter's had gotten snowed in with us the night before. Rob had spent the night on the couch. Later that morning, after breakfast, one of Jaime's indiscretions landed not far from Rob's feet. I apologized, and hastily cleaned up, saying, "He's a horrible dog."

Rob said, in his sweet, observational way, "You guys sure don't like having him around, do you?"

I was startled to hear the truth so baldly stated. "Well," I said, making excuses, feeling guilty, "he's almost fifteen, and he's just a mess. He's already survived two strokes," I added, as though that gave us permission to abuse him verbally.

"Wow," he said. "That's a really long time. I only ever had a dog for five years."

That's when the enormity of my bad behavior hit me. Here I was, a thoughtful, careful mother, an animal lover who cuts apart the plastic rings from soda six-packs so as not to endanger the dolphins, a good Catholic who *writes essays* about raising compassionate children, treating my own dog like dirt. Not only that, I was modeling all the wrong moves for my children and my children's friends: nice going! The more unpleasant I was to Jaime, the more I heard my meanness echoing in their own sharp words to him.

Bless me, Father, for I have sinned.

Rob, bless his heart, has forced me to reappraise my superficial respect for life. It is easy to take a pro-life stand when everyone you care about is healthy and flourishing. It is easy to be against abortion when your children are all wanted and healthy. It is easy to be against euthanasia when your loved ones are thinking and breathing on their own. It is easy to be against the death penalty when you have never been battered by violence. It is easy to open your arms and your heart when things are going well.

Granted, Jaime is a dog, not an elder, but the way his failings have angered me gives me insight into those who lose patience, seemingly unforgivably, with the senile or the faltering patients in their care. In the face of a poor quality of life, it is easy to rationalize that maybe some lives really aren't worth living. What could possibly be the point of severe intellectual disability, of physical paralysis, of mental incapacitation, of terminal illness? Wouldn't these people all be better off dead, in the arms of our eternal God?

Luckily, it is not up to me to determine the point of the lives of others. The picture is a bigger one than I, or any one of us, can see. Each life interconnects with so many others, in so many ways, that determining the value of any link is impossible. On the level of a beating heart, of the divine gift of life, each one of us is equally meaningful and blessed. Some of us may achieve more money or fame or square footage or beauty or children or friends than others; some of us may seem to contribute little of worth. But each of us has the same immortal soul.

Which brings me back to Jaime. Even though I know he does not have a human soul, he has brought us humans affection and warmth. He has taught us gratitude and enthusiasm and devotion. The duration of his canine existence is up to us, as is the quality of his final days. I wish he would die quietly in his sleep, but from past experience with pets, I know that we will more than likely have to fill out the papers and take him for his final shot.

With a small portion of compassion on the part of his human family, however, his time can be lived out, if not fragrantly, at least with dignity and love.

The Prodigal Daughter

(2019)

"Then let us celebrate with a feast, because this son of mine was dead and has come to life again; he was lost, and has been found." (Luke 15:23-24)

Like many of Jesus' parables, the parable of the prodigal son in the Gospel of Luke features an all-male cast. There is the father, loving and merciful, the older son, judgmental and testy, and the younger son, thoughtless and hedonistic. By several homilists over the years, I have been encouraged to cast myself in the role appropriate to my own behavior, with the goal of gaining insight into the practice of my faith.

In my real-life family right now, however, the pertinent roles are female. My husband is a loving father, but recent family matters concern the women.

New insight came upon me when I went to Mass with one of my sisters last month. Again prompted by the homily to cast ourselves as one of the characters in the parable, we talked in the car afterwards. "I'm afraid I'm the older son," my sister said, which is how I have always characterized myself. (My lifelong battle with being super-judgy has yet to be won.) But then my sister said, "I'm the kid who always did the right thing, and I resented it when the kids doing the bad stuff didn't get in trouble!" She admitted that when she was younger, she would have enjoyed seeing those misbehaving kids pay. Her words struck me. I suddenly realized that I completely identify with the prodigal son's father.

I totally get how relieved and joyful that father was to see his returning son "still a long way off," because I've been there. There was a dark time in one of my children's lives when I dreaded answering a call from an unknown number on my phone. Dread is too mild a word, actually, because I was deeply afraid that some unwelcome call was going to notify me that my daughter was dead. A practicing alcoholic, she was out there, at the world's mercy, her behavior rash and risky, and there was nothing I could do about it. When the call finally came, it was less-bad news: she was not dead but in jail. Among other charges, she had assaulted a police officer and destroyed the interior of a police vehicle.

I tell this story with my daughter's permission, because she is now sober. She was lost and now, one day at a time, has been found. Like the father in the story, I have surely celebrated her return from the dead. I have wanted to put a ring on her finger and sandals on her feet. I see with the father's eyes. He was merciful and compassionate, but mostly he was overcome with the relief of not having to bury a beloved child. I get this in my bones.

But my joy is tempered by the way this hopeful new chapter in my daughter's life has given rise to some resentment among her siblings. It's as though they were used to her being the one who messed up all the time, who caused their parents all the grief, and now they don't quite know what to make of her. And as much as she presents this new, improved, self-aware person to them, as much as she wants them to trust her sobriety and integrity and honesty, they don't. Not yet anyway—which she, in turn, does not understand. Why are they so judgmental? Why do they brush her aside so dismissively? Why are they holding on to their expectation of a return to her past prodigal ways?

The brothers in the story do not seem to have been close. My children have been. They have different personalities, but they have always supported each other, a steadfast squad of blood siblings. Now there is turmoil amongst them, as this changing family dynamic rocks everybody's place within it. Don't ever let anyone say that sobriety is easy on a family: the return of a prodigal can spark consuming fires. In the Gospel story, the loving father is the one who tries to bridge the empathy gap between the siblings. I assume that is now my role; the problem is that I don't know if it works. Jesus' story ends before we learn if the father's efforts at reconciliation have been successful. Does the older brother set aside his bitterness and join the feast celebrating his brother's return? Or does he keep himself apart, stuck in all-consuming judgment and antipathy?

I am not some wise person adept at mending the rifts among my children. Since another of my sisters no longer speaks to me, I am obviously not an expert in sorting out the problems siblings may have with each other. I am myself a broken link in a broken chain. My heart hurts at the divisions among my kids, and I pray to find the words and the wisdom to be the bridge, or at least the water they can each safely fall into as they try to cross. (My metaphors are getting a little crazy.) But the next time a homilist suggests that I cast myself in the Gospel reading, I will know that I am no longer the older sibling in the story. God help me, I am the parent.

Illness, Physical and Mental

The Pain and Point of Suffering

(2014)

Every blues musician knows that it's the suffering that gives voice to the blues. But really, suffering goes along with being human. Even the most seemingly charmed life endures its times of suffering, be they great or trifling, spiritual or physical, brief or extended, temporary or final.

Let's face it: we avoid suffering. No one wants to suffer. We want life to be pretty and rosy. We shy away from pain or disappointment or disillusionment. We seek escape in alcohol or drugs, material gain or food. We chase the elusive concept of happiness, which we are certain is just over the next rise.

We also avoid others when they are suffering. We keep them at a distance, as though they are contagious. We would like a hand sanitizer for real life. When someone is grieving, we say things like, "I never know what to say." We don't want to say the wrong thing. And so we say nothing to that someone who could probably really use a sympathetic listener or an accommodating shoulder on which to cry. We cross the street or go down a different aisle at the grocery store to miss the encounter. We dread the face of suffering.

As Christians, we even gloss over Jesus' suffering. Jesus was mocked and abandoned, abused and put to death in a horrible form of capital punishment. We know all that; yet we sometimes turn the cross on which he was crucified into tattoos and jewelry. There's some avoidance.

But the fact of suffering is inescapable. The early Christians exemplify our moral duty to walk with each other in our suffering. The apostles gathered together and suffered the loss of Jesus as a community. We, too, are called to sit with those in pain, to deal with loss and hurt together. When we suffer communally, we take comfort in the faith that has come to us through the ages. We remind ourselves that the resurrected Jesus has sent the Holy Spirit to be with us, on good days and bad.

A father of a kidnapped schoolgirl in Nigeria, reflecting on the dreadful wait to get his daughter back safely, having his hopes raised and then dashed repeatedly, said, "I have died and resurrected many times." This struck me as a profound statement about suffering: we suffer, and we are relieved of suffering, and we are joyful, even though we know we will suffer again. Perhaps the experience of suffering makes our joy that much more precious.

Suffering in itself is not good. Suffering can challenge our faith, even rob us of faith, or make us angry with God. We ask: What kind of God allows a virus to kill us or terrorists to behead us? How does a loving God stand by while hunger and cancer, violence and injustice, betrayal and heartbreak, plague us? We don't have satisfactory answers to these questions. They perplex us and trouble us, even as we recognize that we cannot know the mind of God. All we can know is that God accompanies us in our darkness and misery and pain, that God loves us and is present to us, that God's will for us is good.

When we accept the suffering that comes with our human nature, we give ourselves over to God's will. Is this not the holy act that we pray for daily when we say "Thy will be done"? Jesus, who taught us this prayer, is the ultimate role model for surrendering oneself to God's will, even though for him it meant a torturous death. Jesus knows exactly what human suffering feels like, because he lived it.

When we follow Jesus today, the odds are that we will not be called to suffer mortal martyrdom for our faith. Our martyrdom is more likely metaphorical; it is smaller and less dramatic, but nevertheless meaningful if we live the gospel in our daily lives, and if we unite our personal suffering to the cross. This is the suffering that can transform us. In our brokenness, God's grace can make us whole. This is how we learn compassion. This is how we learn to accompany each other.

It's even how we earn the right to sing the blues.

Mental Health Challenges

(2004)

Three scenarios from the everyday . . .

ONE: My sister tells me that a member of our family is drinking again. He has quit drinking so many times that we have lost count; his cycle is excruciatingly repetitive. He drinks and then drinks heavily; he alienates his family; he becomes paranoid; he starts dropping the balls of adult life; he loses his job; he drinks so much that he is incapacitated and becomes frightened about his health; he seeks out a detox program that helps him to live through his withdrawal symptoms; he gets sober. And each time, it's going to be different. He embodies the apology that the nuns taught us, in the olden days, to say at the end of our trembling-in-the-dark confession: *I am sorry for having offended God and I resolve never to offend Him again.* Except that he doesn't believe in God. He also doesn't believe he needs help.

He doesn't believe he has a disease that, unless and until he admits that he is powerless over its grip and finds someone or something to help him break free of it, is going to kill him. He believes that, with enough willpower and white-knuckling, he can beat his alcoholism. Each time, he gradually pulls himself up by his bootstraps, takes a lot of vitamins, gets another job, either tries to pay off his debts or declares bankruptcy, and convinces his family that he is not a monster of unpredictability. Then he starts jonesing. The insidious alcoholic snake in his brain convinces him that he has somehow become the kind of guy who can enjoy a beer or two on the weekend, a regular guy who can use alcohol in a regular, recreational way. He drinks. And the cycle begins anew.

TWO: One of my daughters is not doing well in high school. After the promise of a stellar freshman year, she is an under-achieving sophomore. Her grades have suffered. Her attitude has deteriorated. She has dropped out of her honors classes and has begun to cut all of her classes without remorse. She has a boyfriend who is too old for her. When my husband and I, in a united front, take away privileges and ground her, which we know are the proper parental measures to take, she runs away and leaves a vaguely suicidal note.

This is our first indication that we are perhaps not dealing with run-of-the-mill teenage angst and rebellion, as we did with her siblings before her. We are frightened. When she comes home, we turn to a family therapist, where we endure enlightening and painful sessions. I start to get the tiniest bit of a clue that the anxiety and depression my daughter lives with on a daily basis are far more difficult than anything I have ever undergone emotionally. My occasional negative feelings are transitory, a nuisance that can usually be swept aside with a cup of hot tea. Hers are ever-present, debilitating, crippling, deeply scary. She needs more than all the tea in the world. And I have no idea how to cure her.

THREE: The mother of a former confirmation student, whom I have not seen since my youth ministry days at the church, calls to request a favor. *Have I seen the paper?* she asks.

I have. The news is pretty sensational for a small town: her son, my former student, has been convicted of child molestation, on the strength of the testimony of a six-year-old girl. I remember her son as a typical kid, more racist than most teenagers, but a pretty normal, football-playing, agreeable, spiritually apathetic boy. I have not seen him for at least five years, but I have heard rustlings that he has had some issues with drugs and anger. Now the newspaper. Now the six-year-old girl.

I know that he is almost due for sentencing. I also know that both his mother and father are correctional officers employed at the local state prison, and so have no illusions about the place where their son is probably going. As the son of guards, on top of being a convicted child molester, he is headed for a world of trouble.

So I am not surprised when his mother wants me to write a letter on her son's behalf, a sort of character reference, for his defense lawyer to use to plead for leniency, for probation instead of prison time. She tells me the long sad story of her son's innocence, of the trumped-up charges against him, how he was told that the only way to avoid prison time was to own up to his transgressions, that the six-year-old girl, the daughter of his girlfriend, was coached by the cops, was confused, was only six years old, for God's sake, and eventually would have agreed with whatever depravity they suggested to her, just so they would stop asking her questions.

The mother is hoping for a mistrial, hoping to erase the whole incident so that her son will not have to register as a sex offender for the rest of his life, hoping that all can be made well, and I have no way to fathom the depth of her denial. I don't know what is factual and what is desperation.

I tell her that I have not had any contact with her son for a long time, and she says that's all right; just write about what he was like when he was in high school. She is eager for whatever crumbs I might drop her way. It seems that I am one of the few people in town who will even talk to her: teachers, counselors, and coaches will not return her calls or e-mails. She has only a few days left to gather these testimonies. I agree to help, but I say it will be brief.

So, what to write? I empathize with a mother wanting only to protect her son from harm; I also empathize with six-year-old girls who are victimized by and need protection from predators. I don't know if this boy-man is guilty or innocent. I finally write a lukewarm, sketchy letter. I say he was a reliable altar boy. I say he was no trouble on field trips. I say he had good attendance. What good can this letter do? Because I can't speak to his heart or soul.

When we think of visiting the sick, we picture cancer patients, or old people with walkers, or car accident victims: at least I do. We bring them soup or flowers; we take Communion to them. They are physically sick, and some of them will get better. Far more difficult is the task of visiting with those who are mentally or emotionally or spiritually sick. They tend not to be people whom we seek out, but family members and friends who are, for better or for worse, in our lives, those who make us lose our patience, who drive us crazy. My alcoholic relative makes me want to take him by the shoulders and shake some sense into him, but I have to remind myself to breathe. I have to try to be understanding and supportive, and to realize that he is as sick as someone with a brain tumor. I have to hope that this time really will be different. With my daughter, I can spot a down day the moment she wakes up, and I want to run from the house, because, God forgive me, I sometimes find her depressions so *tiring*. But I stay, scramble her some eggs, lend an ear if she feels like talking. The mother of the perhaps-unjustly-convicted child molester makes me want to stop answering the phone, to screen my calls, to pretend I never got her message. I don't really want to get stuck in her messy web of legality and panic. But she is doing what mothers do, standing by her son, fighting for his rights, and whether he is guilty or not, her son needs somebody's help.

These are people who are sick, who are in pain, and even though I cannot fix them, they are still my responsibility. It is up to me to be present to them, if only to demonstrate in a small way that God has not forgotten them, that God hears them, and that God will never abandon them. On bad days, I might like to. But God does not abandon me, either, and so I am called to summon that lingering shred of compassion, that tentative outstretched hand, that slow-moving smile. And offer all that I can.

Panic

(2021)

At first they only happened when I was driving. Which was not a good thing. I'd have my two babies strapped into their car seats, all safe and sound, on our way to the grocery store or to their little pottery class, and the panic would creep over me: vision blurring, breath shortening, heart beating faster, head swooning, skin clamming, heart pounding nearly out of my chest, a full-on attack. The first time it happened I thought I was having a heart attack, even though I was still in my twenties. Or maybe some strange force was crushing my lungs. I was afraid I was going to die, so I pulled over before I also killed my children. Then I waited to die. But the symptoms subsided. The vise loosened its grip. My racing heart slowed, then began to beat normally. The dizziness disappeared. I was all right. My life would go on.

After surviving several of these scary incidents, I realized that my heart was not really giving out, because the attacks only happened when there wasn't another adult in the car. Or in the house. In retrospect, I recognize that they stemmed from the fact that I felt alone and overwhelmed. I had two small children and another on the way. Although my husband was busy at work and took on extra work, we had money problems. I felt guilty that I was not bringing in a paycheck. But I was carrying the whole family. I was exhausted, but I rarely slept well.

I told no one about these panic attacks, not my husband, not my mother, not anyone. I was embarrassed to admit that I was not Super Mom. Panic attacks are well-named for the instant and irrational fear they escort into any random moment, but by then I'd done enough research to feel comfortable that I knew what they were. It wasn't my heart failing, it was my head. It was my psyche. With each attack, I held on tight to the knowledge that the attack would end. I would keep breathing, and I would survive. The attacks became a bit like old friends who visited at inconvenient times. They continued through the birth of my third child. Sometimes when the walls were closing in, I was afraid I would drop the new baby. Somehow, I didn't. The new baby was colicky and cranky, which in hindsight I attribute to the precarious condition of her mother's mental health. It must have been a stressful time for all my children.

My ability to cope as a mother deteriorated. I became pretty sure that I actually was slowly dying, that my darlings wouldn't even remember their dead mother. When my erratically beating heart finally drove my husband to take me to the doctor, however, I was diagnosed with "combat fatigue." The doctor told my husband that I needed rest. I needed support. I needed to care for my own shaky health. To make a long, difficult story shorter: Under God's gentle care and with the help of a book on co-dependence and a disciplined self-help program, I got better. I learned to pace myself and ask for help when I needed it. I slept more soundly. My husband faced and wrestled with his own demons and became a more attentive partner and parent. Daily life with all its stresses got easier as we grew more open with each other. We became a team. The attacks mostly stopped.

I didn't tell my husband about the panic attacks for a long time. I didn't tell anybody. And it's made me realize that we really do feel ashamed of mental health problems. I wasn't actually dying, but I was sick. It was just the wrong kind of sickness. It felt like weakness. It felt like a deep deficiency in me. It felt like something that should be kept secret. Why do we persist in this belief?

My kids are grown now and have all been in therapy at one point or another. They have pulled through some dicey times, which makes me glad that being in therapy, a practice that was less common, or at least less discussed, when I was young has largely lost its stigma. Self-help books and groups and sponsors and meetings do us a lot of good on the road to wellness. Yet we still strive to pretend to be OK, to seem OK, even when we are not. We cover up our deficiencies. We don't show our brokenness and our scars. We are not good at asking for help.

Maybe we also aren't good at perceiving when someone needs help. No one in my family, not my husband, not my parents, not my siblings, ever noticed what a mess I was during my darkest times. I suppose I was an accomplished actress. Whenever I have told any one of them that I am a grizzled veteran of panic attacks, they are shocked.

And I am no better. My daughter who is pregnant with her first child lives in another state. I think of her and worry about her and pray for her all the time. But recently she hesitated before saying on the phone, "Mom, I wish you'd check in on me more."

My first reaction was, "What are you talking about?" My inner defensive players lined up for the snap. Was she saying I was inadequate, or thoughtless, or a bad mother? But after a moment, what I said was only, "I can do that." Because I realized that she was bravely doing that very hard thing to do: she was asking for help. And I can help. It's not difficult to make time for others, to reach out for the few minutes it takes to send a text or make a call to the people we love. Being conscious of their needs is the tricky part.

The doctor who diagnosed my combat fatigue all those years ago may never know that he changed the course of my life, that he prompted a sea change in our marriage and our coparenting, that my mental health has maintained a balance, that rather than getting progressively worse, my panic attacks subsided. He saw a woman who needed help, and he helped her, even though she didn't know how to ask. Another lesson in grace.

Careers/Money

Failure High: My First and Last Year of Teaching

(2006–2007)

In one hour, I became a high school English teacher. I was interviewed at 9:00 a.m. and hired at 10:00. By 11:00, I was attending an orientation session for new teachers at the district office, my mind swimming in a surreal sea. Classes started in one week.

A writer by vocation, I'd been a substitute teacher by paycheck. But circumstances had changed, and so, as I approached my 50th birthday, I found myself taking college classes to earn my California clear credential alongside fellow students who were the ages of my children. I had been hired as an "intern" teacher, which meant that I could work full-time as a paid teacher as long as I was chipping away at those required classes.

The circumstances? My husband, with my encouragement, had left a high-paying, soul-sucking administrative job to become a professor of education, to teach new teachers. He had wanted to teach at the university level ever since he had earned his doctorate, and a job opened up suddenly. The new position, while on a tenure track, was a 30% cut in pay. This was serious money to a man with four kids and a wife working as a sporadically hired substitute and a sporadically paid writer. I wrote a weekly newspaper column, but since I was not selling any blockbuster novels, I needed to follow Plan B to punch up our combined income. I had figured for many years that if it became necessary, I could always teach.

I could always teach. Many of us assume that if our real lives don't work out, we can always settle for the security of a job for which there will always be a demand, as long as people insist on procreating. I could teach. What was so hard about teaching? I'd watched my husband do it in elementary classrooms for years.

My hasty interview had materialized through one of my husband's coworkers: a public high school that was located on an Air Force base needed an English teacher fast, and I needed a job. I think they hired a writer with the hopeful expectation that the students' writing skills would benefit from being taught by someone who actually wrote.

We'd see about that.

At the orientation, I filled out forms. My employment was contingent on whether I was telling the truth about not being a convicted felon, and about never having been charged with the abuse or molestation of a minor. I was briefed on how to report suspected child abuse, how to deal with special education needs, how to avoid the blood and other bodily fluids that might spew from a student. I had to be fingerprinted, photographed, contracted, documented in triplicate. In exchange, I would be given a more substantial paycheck than I had ever earned in my life and a dazzling array of cost-free benefits for me and my family.

Teacher's Journal Entry, August 16:

My first full day as an English teacher. What kind of teacher is bored on her first day of prep because she has nothing to do?

I covered the dilapidated bulletin boards with purple paper, since the school colors are purple and white. I made name tags. I read through the first few grammar lessons: verbs and more verbs. Now I'm watching the clock.

When I went to get my military ID this morning, I got lost. I drove miles into the desert, into the underbelly of the base, looking for a street that doesn't exist in spite of Google Maps. When I tried to call the school for directions, I realized that my cell phone does not work on base. My only option was to stop at a squat, lone building that said COMBAT TRAINING. "What can I help you with, ma'am?" asked an alarmed young man in camouflage, as an entire roomful of camouflage turned to stare at me. Was I possibly an unannounced lesson in how to deal with a harmless-looking terrorist?

"I think I'm lost," I said, and told the young man where I was trying to go.

"Oh, you are lost," he said, in a somber tone that made me glad he was not my pastor. "But it's easy enough to get back," he added, filling me with hope. I arrived at my appointment with one minute to spare. I'm glad I have my father's genes and allowed extra time for something bad to happen: traffic, a flat tire, a wrong turn, the apocalypse.

Even though I'd been a substitute for years, the reality that these people were counting on me to teach a whole bunch of teenagers, 125 of them with hard-to-learn names and diverse personalities and surprisingly heavy emotional baggage, enough English (reading and writing, grammar and vocabulary) to score well on the state tests, and to keep them under control whenever they were in my classroom, quickly seemed an insurmountable challenge. After about three polite days of classes, the students figured out that not only did I not know what I was doing academically, I was also a dismal disciplinarian.

And then it was *on*. In Room 6, the inmates were running the asylum. A kid came to class drunk and I didn't even recognize the signs: I'd believed he was loopy and had to keep his sunglasses on because he had a migraine. I lost two kids during a fire drill. Several kids pointed out that I didn't seem to know much about teaching, about how a classroom works. Kids who refused to do any work faced me down. I ate a layer cake of failure. With apologies to Jerry Maguire, I didn't need a jacket. I was *cloaked* in failure.

My students didn't like grammar, didn't see the *point*. My students talked too much, and even though I sometimes liked talking with them, I worried about having no control. Was it sharing or was it out of hand? Were they learning a damn thing or was I ineffectual? Worse: although I totally understood infinitives, knew them in my cells and in my bones, why was I finding them so difficult to explain?

The principal visited every now and then, poking his inscrutable face into the room, showing neither encouragement nor alarm, and leaving as soon as the inevitable every-five-minute emergency squawked over his walkie-talkie. He didn't fire me, which I took as a positive sign. Then again, they'd had a hard enough time finding even someone as unqualified as I to take this job.

It seemed that the kids who understood grammar came in the door already understanding and were bored by the review. The kids who didn't get it didn't really care. I felt that I was constantly trying to hide my inexperience as well as the fact that I didn't really care if they got it either. I lacked the soul of a teacher. Rather than trying to find a way into their minds, I just wanted them to stay alive and unhurt until the bell rang. I just wanted us all to emerge unscathed by our time together.

Perhaps my minimalist classroom helped to give me away. I tried to act like it was purposefully Zen rather than fraudulent. But I didn't have any *stuff*. I didn't have inspirational posters or framed sayings or a globe or even a collection of pencils sticking out of a mug that said "If You Can Read This, Thank A Teacher." I hadn't earned any teacher stuff. Heck, I didn't even have a *credential*. I had the stapler and the tape that came with the desk, and a box of tissues that the secretary in the office had given me. The first time my college teaching advisor visited my classroom to observe me, he pronounced my room "barren."

"Put up some student work!" he exclaimed. "Show them you care!" Old coot, I thought. But I had the kids make posters about the parts of speech using old magazines and glitter, which did brighten the place up.

As well as take up an entire class period.

I was running out of things to do. When I was hired, the head of the English department told me that he provided the syllabus and lesson plans for all the English classes, so I didn't have to worry about those things. This seemed like a good deal to me. Except that once we were several weeks into the quarter and I had almost gone through the initial plans he gave me, which covered phrases and clauses in grammar, he became elusive. It didn't help my reputation as a rookie when students asked me what books we would be reading this year, and I didn't actually know. What was after grammar? *Uh, I don't know.* Were we doing any research papers? *Uh, do you usually?* I sent the department head e-mails inquiring about a syllabus or lesson plans. I sent him my student helpers with notes, asking for a syllabus or lesson plans. As time went on and we completed the grammar units, I went to his room myself, begging for anything: a syllabus, lesson plans, some guidance. This guy was supposed to be my intern coach, a responsibility for which he received a stipend, and he avoided me like spam. He finally gave me a few guidelines for essays: descriptive, reflective, expository, opinion. It was something to do, but it wasn't enough. I struck out into uncharted territory, with no clear idea of where the state of California wanted me to end up.

Finally, I did what the head of the department had told me was an utter waste of time: I had all the kids bring in a notebook in which to journal. For five minutes at the beginning of every class, we all wrote on a given topic or on whatever topic we wanted in our journals. I told them the words between the covers of their journals were uncensored. I told them that although I would occasionally read their entries, they would receive a grade for the act of writing, not for the content. I told them that writing time was sacred time for me, and that I required absolute silence. They fell for it; for five minutes a day, anyway, their pencils were moving. For some of them, it was the best, most honest, most thoughtful work they did all year.

Teacher's Journal Entry, September 11:
9-11, five years later, and who would have ever thought I'd be teaching on an Air Force base? Who would have ever thought? I feel like I am walking on foreign soil—a closet dissenter teaching the children of the most loyal, the most unquestioning, the most willing to sacrifice for God and country. I am curious about the backgrounds of these students, about their dinner table conversations, about the values they soak in on a daily basis. The students are funny about 9-11, almost as though they don't get all the fuss. They were so young, and perhaps unmarked by the memory of violence so far away.

My high school students were Pavlovian: when the dismissal bell from any period was precisely five minutes away, they salivated. They lost all focus. They started to pack up their things, gabbing and acting like class was over. "But the bell's gonna ring!" they said if I mentioned that we were still work-

ing. "The bell's gonna ring!" Once, I kept a class for two minutes after the bell rang, two minutes into lunch, just to make
a point. But the point I wanted to make, I didn't make. I simply
proved that if students were Pavlovian, teachers were power-
mad. Our power was absolute, and we sometimes used it vin-
dictively, blindly, without even remembering what the point
was that we thought we had to make.

Teaching seemed to coax out the authoritarian, sarcastic
witch in me, which made me realize more than ever that I was
a writer, not a teacher. Writing made sense. Writing made me
feel alive and functional. Teaching made me think about how
peaceful death might be.

Going back to college for the credential program was the
clincher: I had made a big mistake. I had no interest in, or
patience with, the intellectual discipline of teaching. I was a
fish out of water in the education system. I flopped and gasped,
despairing of ever getting back to the blue, blue sea. A fish
cannot go to school to learn how to be a goat or a bird. A fish
cannot learn to gallop or fly. Fish gotta swim.

Timewise, I couldn't keep up with the required work. I was
having a difficult enough time keeping up with my weekly
column deadlines and had even skipped a week in order to
catch up on grading papers. The worst college assignment was
having to listen to a tape of me teaching my sixth period class,
and then writing an evaluation of myself. I considered getting
out the thesaurus to look up synonyms for *stink, dismal,* and
hopeless so I wouldn't overuse those words.

My teaching advisor, whose job was to observe me and then
spell out everything I was terrible at, as if that weren't painfully
evident, asked me about the rest of my life. I began to tell him:
I had four children; I wrote two columns; I taught confirmation classes at my church; I volunteered at the state prison . . .

"Stop, stop!" he said, covering his ears. "You're making me tired just listening to this!" He told me that if I expected to complete the credential program, I would have to give all of that up. Well, maybe not the offspring. But absolutely everything else.

I was unconvinced. I had no wish to give up any of these parts of me. I slogged on through the first quarter, publishing what were essentially rough drafts of columns, teaching, grading, going to my evening classes, neglecting my family. One evening, during the beginning teaching seminar, my advisor said offhandedly to another student, "No one goes into teaching for the *money*. If that's why you teach, you should *not* be a teacher."

Everyone laughed. But I froze, stunned. He was right. And there I was, teaching *for the money*. I was doing the teaching profession a huge disservice by passing myself off as a teacher. I was a fraud. I was in the wrong place. And I knew it.

An incredible peace came over me once I decided to flunk my two college classes: I, who had graduated from college as class salutatorian and who had considered a B+ a kind of character weakness. I would not be able to retain my intern credential once I was out of university, but I could technically take a temporary leave of absence for two quarters and thereby manage to teach until the end of the school year. I dropped out, an embarrassment to my professor husband, who could not imagine that anyone, especially his wife, would not *love* being a teacher.

Getting an F was painful, let alone two. But it was also strangely liberating. The first time I told my advisor that I had not done an assignment, I took a lesson from my non-working students, and when he interrogated me with that intimidating, disapproving teacher look, I *faced him down*. For the first time in my life, I really did not care what someone thought of me.

In all my years of school, I had never not done an assignment. I don't think I ever even turned in anything late. But I was too tired. I just plain hadn't had time to complete it, and I didn't bother making an excuse. I also, for the first time ever, did not internalize another person's disapproval. I may have been cloaked in failure, but I was somehow wickedly calm. I was learning how to wear failure, but with style.

Teacher's Journal Entry, November 2:
Having one of those days when I look at all these faces, and I just want to say, "Forget it. I can't do this. I don't know what I'm talking about." And leave. They can manage without me. I have a heavy, heavy period and so all of my focus is on cramps and making it successfully to the bathroom between classes. That's pretty much what's going on with me. I am hating my job today.

Sometimes students remind me of my own kids and so they break my heart. One girl reminds me of my oldest daughter, so emphatic, so emotional, so wide-open to damage. I want to protect her. I want to pray for her. I have to stop, or I really will cry in front of all these faces.

My impersonation of an English teacher dragged on through the fall.

Each week, my students were supposed to memorize the definitions of ten vocabulary words. The words were pulled from the approved-by-the-state-of-California literature textbook but were assigned to them as an alphabetized list of 100 words. In the textbook, the words were presented in groups that had something to do with a particular selection. They were to be learned, and perhaps remembered, within a literary context. This made more sense to me than the disembodied list, but the head of the English department insisted that the list be presented as he had typed it however-many years ago, and each weekly test was to be cumulative. In other words, by the tenth week of the semester, my students were supposed to be able to spit out 100 definitions of words they were unlikely ever to adopt as their own.

So on Mondays, my students wrote out the ten new words with their definitions taken from the back of the literature book—brief, sketchy definitions that were sometimes incomplete. This became clear when I asked the students to use their new words in sentences showing that they understood the words' meanings. (No fair writing the sentence, "Howard knew what the word <u>boisterous</u> meant.") But the troubling textbook definitions were often misleading. For example, for the adjective "base," the textbook offered the definition "lowly," which led to student-created sentences like: "I like the bottom bunk because it is <u>base</u>." A bad definition was almost worse than no definition. Even the careful underlining of the new word did not help it to make any sense.

Sometimes I had to un-teach things they had actually learned, as when a few students were genuinely surprised to see that the correct spelling of the word "ludicrous" was not "Ludacris."

My favorite desperate, made-up definition on a test, the result of some careful etymological reasoning: "morass: having a bigger butt than normal." (I gave half-credit for creativity.)

So every Monday: definitions and sideways sentences. Then I came up with the stellar idea of flashcards. I requisitioned some index cards from the office. Then I spent a chunk of change on an enormous classroom supply, because I wanted to be sure that no one had the excuse of not having index cards. After a while, kids started asking me for extras, which I eventually learned were for Biology class, whose experienced teacher smartly assigned them to bring index cards from home. I hadn't thought of that.

The thing was, the only kids who made and studied the flashcards were the kids who would have studied the words just from their initial lists anyway. The ones with the flashcards didn't need the flashcards. This was true of every assignment I ever gave: the kids who completed the work already mostly knew the information anyway, while the kids who were the most unschooled made sure that they remained that way. It wasn't just that they were inattentive; it was as though they actively blocked information from entering their brains. They did little classwork, no homework, flunked their vocab quizzes, and really didn't care what points they missed as a result. They fell further and further behind, so that, by the end of ten weeks, they really did need to learn 100 words in order to pass, rather than simply the last ten.

"Ms. Schultz, what does 'futile' mean?" asked one of my underachieving students, about five minutes before the final 100-word test. He pronounced the unfamiliar word with a long "i" sound: "few-tile."

Exactly, I almost said.

Look in the mirror, I almost said.

"It means 'hopeless,'" I finally said. "Without purpose."

Kind of like our vocabulary tests.

I tried to make the tests more interesting, and a bit easier, than the ones given to me by the department head, which consisted of a well-spaced list of the vocab words with the instruction: "Define the following words." I made some sections exercises in matching. I created crossword puzzles. I composed weirdly compelling sentences with blanks into which the proper vocabulary word was to be inserted. Creating the Friday test during my prep period was actually the most fun I had all week as a teacher. I could have written tests all day. Which was one more small indication that I really was not where I was supposed to be.

Christmas showered me with the gifts of teaching: My sixth period class gave me a thank-you card that they had all signed with little notes of good wishes, and my worst-behaved student from third period hugged me twice. I received several presents, some odd-smelling body lotions, and a packet of what looked like secondhand stationery, a bit crumpled and faded, which made me regret every re-gifted item my own children had ever presented to a teacher. We had organized class potlucks since the last day before the holiday break was a shortened school day, during the course of which I had to eat a whole plate of banana pudding studded with vanilla wafers and whipped cream, and a hefty serving of a peculiar mixture of orange Jell-O, cottage cheese, sour cream, cool whip, and mandarin oranges. Both of these delicacies were concocted and presented by very proud boys, and I just didn't have the heart to say that: 1) I hate banana pudding, and 2) I don't eat gelatin because I am a vegetarian. I swallowed my preferences and my principles along with the banana pudding dream and the orange Jell-O surprise. My stomach bothered me all afternoon. But my conscience did not.

I read my students' journal descriptions of "An Early Christmas Memory" over the winter holiday, and some of them bit into my heart with tiny teeth. "This was the very best Christmas I ever had, mainly cause my family was together," wrote one. "This was back when things were perfect," wrote another. They vaguely described the holiday anticipation and the gifts, but they pined in detail for two parents in one bed, for jumping on a mom and a dad to wake them up in the early morning, or else snuggling into the bed of an intact marriage. They were so wistful for the time when their parents were still together. I wondered if parents would work harder on salvage if they could magically read the pain with which their future teenagers would write.

"Christmas smells like old people and firewood," wrote another student, thus curing my romanticism.

A fascinating aspect of teaching on a military base, besides base exercises and Delta alerts, which involve soldiers with guns and which really gum up the flow of commuter traffic onto and off of the base, was that the students were relentlessly mobile. Every three years, some of them were uprooted in the middle of the school year and roughly transplanted, sometimes into the soil of places like Japan or Iceland. New students arrived all the time, and old ones unceremoniously left. "I'm moving to Spain/Florida/Guam tomorrow," kids would announce matter-of-factly. But the way they dealt with their lot in life was a miracle of the military: they were unfailingly open to and accepting of new kids, because they all knew what it was like to be the new kid with that tentative, deer-in-the-headlights look, plopped into the middle of a school year at a new school. They were kind and careful with each other, and there was a near absence of cliquish exclusion and racial tension. I sometimes thought that this small public high school on a military base was a microcosm of an ideal, egalitarian society, and its occupants didn't even realize the magic they had conjured.

I always wanted to say to the new kids that I knew exactly how they felt, but I knew it would ring false: I was the teacher. I was another species.

Teacher's Journal Entry, January 10:
We are writing about the nicest thing we've ever done, and one of my students is concerned that it's bad luck to write down the nicest thing you've ever done, because if you talk about it, maybe its niceness won't count in your cosmic favor in the afterlife. I told him that writing it is not the same as telling it, as though I have some sort of insight into the mind and/or operating system of God. Then this kid threw a soda at another kid, which was definitely not the nicest thing he'd ever done, and the paper towels he fetched from the boys' bathroom had the absorbency of a stone.

It's a new year.

At the end of the first semester, I had several students who knew they deserved to flunk English. The sun broke out and shone in their faces when they got news of a D-minus. A D-minus! Who gets excited over that? But it meant they wouldn't have to endure all of this again in summer school. I didn't flunk anyone: the D-minus kids did very little work, and did nothing energetically or well, but they at least gave me something to grade. The only kid I would have flunked, because he did, literally, *nothing*, moved to Washington at Christmas time. The heartening thing was, once the new semester began, my D-minus kids were actually working. It was as though they knew they'd been given a gift, and they were paying it back.

With the new semester came my feeble push into the literature book. The communications blackout within the English department was still in effect, for God knew what reason, other than that the head of the department was either: 1) professionally overcommitted and personally overextended, or 2) a jerk. I browsed through the book and made a list of what I thought we could feasibly cover before the first week of June. About halfway through the semester, a student said, "Ms. Schultz, every time we start a new story, you say it's by your favorite author. They can't *all* be your favorite author!" Which is when I realized that the only criterion I had used, while choosing the selections we would read as a class, were ones that I liked. From the book, I assigned them Flannery O'Connor, Margaret Atwood, Joan Didion, Alice Walker, Tim O'Brien, Truman Capote, and all the Shakespeare contained therein. Since I had become a one-shot teacher, I didn't care what the state standards dictated that we cover. Since I had no syllabus, I created one that offered things that I wanted to read or share. It wasn't the right way to teach; it was a way to survive the year.

Once, a student said, "This is a pretty good story, Ms. Schultz," in a tone of total surprise, as though a pretty good story had no business emerging from the pages of a literature textbook. I felt momentarily hopeful, until another student was kind enough to bring me down from the clouds: "Hey," she asked, "isn't William Faulkner the guy from *Meet the Parents*?"

Another student turned in a paper that discussed the "lamination" in Sophocles's *Antigone*. Despite the description of the wailing and mourning over the tragic and untimely death of Antigone, all I could picture was a group of robed Greek women coating the dead Antigone with a hot thin layer of plastic. The indignity.

Teacher's Journal Entry, February 3:

Last night I dreamt that I kissed a student, which made me feel, upon waking, like one of those female teachers who go to prison for sleeping with a student and then give birth to his love child while incarcerated. I haven't discussed this dream with anyone, because it's freaking me out.

And here I thought I was the grown-up in the classroom. God help me.

There were often outbreaks on campus of what my students referred to as "drama": the hormonal outpourings of large groups of teenagers in daily proximity. One day several girls were crying in two separate classes, and a boy in a third class said in an unaffected way that he was the cause of the tears. Another time, a student asked to switch to another period because she could no longer concentrate in the class where her former best friend now shunned her. Many unexcused tardies, absences, and cuts were attributed to personal (drama) reasons. As a mother of daughters (and as a girl myself in the last century), I was familiar with the two-headed best friend/worst enemy friendships between girls, and the lightning speed with which the relationship could change and change back. I also knew all about boys, about pining for them, despising them, wanting them, fearing them, and even the plain vanilla of simply enjoying their company. But I also knew that, as far as my students were concerned, I was ignorant, blind, and dumb, devoid of any understanding of dating or mating.

Everywhere, between classes, outside the windows, between buildings, teenagers paired off. Young men and women, having discovered that spark, began behaving like adults. They held hands, walked close together, kissed (forbidden on campus), and had small arguments. Their body language sometimes looked so much older than they were, girls slumped in submission, boys putting on airs of domination, both imitating things they had seen and internalized in their young lives. Some days I felt disheartened, just looking out my window at the stereotypical roles being fulfilled. I wanted to say to those girls: *Don't settle! Don't sell yourselves short! You don't need him, even if you've convinced yourself that you do!* And to the boys: *Don't settle! Don't be manipulated! Think with your brain, not your reproductive organs!* And to all: *Teen pregnancy!*

Other times, I was happy for love, wherever it existed. Some of my students seemed to have very little of it in their lives.

Teacher's Journal Entry, March 26:
A new quarter (the LAST one) and once again, as grades come out, the room is full of remorse. Remorse swirls in the air, stains the walls, makes the floor slippery. Remorse oozes from the pores of students who fear the worst: "Did you turn in grades yet?" they want to know, awash in anxiety, dreading the grounding that is sure to come. "Oh yes, grades are turned in." The grading period ended last Friday. Grades permeated my weekend and my brain. And now we are done. A new quarter, virginal and

demure, awaits our efforts and wooing for the next ten weeks.
And then, blessedly, God willing, it will be over.

The week of state testing was unlike any other week: We fed
kids breakfast and supplied #2 pencils with sturdy erasers. We
made sure everybody was in the right place at the right time.
Testing *mattered.* We teachers read the instructions to the tests
like robots, after we'd signed a pledge saying that we would not
reveal anything we saw on any test. Or if we did, they'd have to
kill us: the test materials were state secrets. Some of the kids
tried to do well on the tests, which were more important to the
future well-being and status of the school as a whole than to the
individual student, while some of them colored in patterns of
answer-circles on the answer sheets, or randomly guessed without even reading the questions. Some of them were finished in
a dizzying five minutes, and we had to note their names so that
next year, when parents complained about how badly their kid
did, we could say that the kid obviously didn't try. Once the
morning testing was over, the rest of the day was spent frivo-
lously, watching movies or socializing, and as they left for the
day, we encouraged them to get a good night's sleep that night.

When I was hired, I was told that these test scores would be
my grade as a teacher. I remember feeling nervous about that.
But I had learned how to shrug and say "Whatever" and *mean*
it. I had gotten good at failing.

One of my students thought I spent every journal period
writing down a list of who's bad and who's talking and who
forgot their book. I told him I'd be a pretty bitter person if I
spent five minutes of every hour noting whom I'm mad at and
who's misbehaving. I think he thought teachers were much
more interested in his every move than they actually were. Or
at least than I was. Those five minutes were my tiny thoughtful

times, a time of release and reflection, even if they were inter-rupted by sound effects and annoying whispers. I pulled whole newspaper columns out of five-minute intervals of writing: sort of like time-efficiency ab workouts. I also wrote more than a few columns on teenagers and education, because that was all the raw material I had time for.

Over my year of failure as a teacher, I met some teachers who were successes. They were like my husband: teaching animated them, made them feel like they were doing some-thing essential, that they were serving a purpose. Teaching was the guiding star of their lives, and they spared nothing of themselves in following that light. While I did not avoid my fellow teachers, I did not seek them out. I felt I was an impos-tor who did not belong with them. And I felt unworthy of their company. I knew the steep dues they had paid to be in that group, and I wasn't willing to cough them up. One teacher called me a traitor when he heard I was not returning to teach the following year, only partly in jest. Then he said that if there were anything else he could do as well, he would surely do it.

In my formative years I'd had good teachers, and my chil-dren had had good teachers, but I don't know that I really appreciated all they did until I was in their place. Good teach-ers were sort of like the kids on skateboards who hung around the school parking lot after hours: they made what they did so expertly look effortless. Watching them, you thought you could do what they did, until you actually tried to stay upright atop a thin speeding platform on wheels, let alone zoom through flawless turns and flips. From the humble perspective of falling on your behind, you had a lot more respect.

Teacher's Journal Entry, May 9:

I am tired of dreaming about these kids, of worrying about these kids, of trying to figure these kids out. How do teachers do this for 20 or 30 years, year after year after year, allowing students to take up residence (squatters, really) in their brains? How do they retain any sense of self, or do they willingly give it away? As a first-year teacher, I haven't even had to do the extra-curricular stuff that the other teachers do: coaching, advising, chaperoning, spearheading, serving on committees. They are saints. Wild horses couldn't drag me back for another year.

Also: nothing like announcing there is a SWARM of BEES on campus to settle everybody right down.

At first I was resistant to the humanity of being a teacher. I wanted it all to be about paper and pens. I didn't want any relationship with my students above the ground floor. I didn't go to the football games. I didn't go to the drama club's production of *Little Shop of Horrors*. I had enough horror in my own little shop.

And I didn't really want kids congregating in my classroom at lunchtime, but since I was *there*, eating my yogurt and working the crossword, I really had no excuse to throw them out. It just gradually happened. First a few loner kids came by with their lunch trays, looking for some peace. Then a few girls came for a quiet place to use their phones undisturbed. Then a couple of boys brought chess boards and set up impromptu tournaments. A few more kids brought decks of cards. And a few just really wanted to talk. With me. By the end of my year, I realized that about the only thing I had to offer as a teacher was my humanity. Humanity was my best gift: compassion, and an ear. I didn't have the theory, the technique, the state standards, the classroom discipline skills, the voice, or the repertoire of teacher tools. But I really liked those kids. I'd gotten them under my skin.

Teacher's Journal Entry, June 1:

June! Counting today, five more days of school! This is our last journal entry, and I hope that maybe I have planted some seeds this year. I will never actually know; part of the lovely mystery of life. Sometimes we don't see the circles emanating from the pebble we toss. But that doesn't mean the ripples aren't there. Maybe the nature of faith is understood in the unseen ripples of our tossed pebbles: we believe what we do not see. We sense the presence of something powerful but invisible. Then we continue on as though we do see it.

My year of failure ended with the last final exam and the last bell. My students surged forth joyously to greet the summer, and I totally shared their sense of liberation. I was thankful to have survived the year. But as I sat in my stripped and silent classroom on that last day, I felt a little sad to have flunked as a teacher. I was headed for a less-taxing job in an office, the kind of job you do for eight hours and go home and give no more thought to, exactly the kind of job that would give a writer more time to write, but still. I suddenly understood that I was going to miss my students. I'd been a lousy teacher, but I turned out to be a fairly good traveling companion. I have the little love notes and the recipe for Orange Jell-O/Cottage Cheese Surprise, souvenirs from the journey, to prove it.

The Thinner Wallet
(2009)

My husband and I had to quit the credit card habit cold turkey. Two months ago, we cut up fifteen different cards, all of which have balances that are now in the process of being paid off, courtesy of a debt management company. It's going to take us five years. But we are now a cash-only family.

Sometimes I feel like I'm jonesing, like I need a fix. There's something I can't afford, and I want badly to *charge it*. Kicking the credit card habit is hard, man. I compare giving up my credit cards to an addiction I am familiar with: it's been a lot like quitting smoking.

When I first quit smoking, I felt like I'd lost my best friend. That elegant tube of tobacco gave me peace, gave me security, gave me gratification. Even though I knew in my head that smoking was deadly, in my heart I mourned that lovely rush of nicotine. Now I feel similarly lonely and joyless without my credit cards. Each thin piece of embossed plastic gave me peace, gave me security, gave me gratification. Having a credit card, or in my case a bouquet of credit cards, to pull out of my wallet in an emergency gave me a snug sense of well-being. For parents, it's comforting to know that whatever situation your kid might get into, you can probably charge them out of it. When the unexpected happens, a car emergency or a home maintenance crisis or a family funeral that requires an airline ticket, relief arrives in the form of plastic. I could pay for anything life tossed at me. If I was short on cash—and I was always short on cash—I knew I could charge whatever we needed. The problem would be solved.

Except that our emergencies became more and more frequent, and we charged things that weren't actually emergencies: vacations and prom dresses, theater tickets and nice dinners out. Frivolous things thoughtlessly went on plastic.

Still, we had ridiculously high credit limits that we would surely never reach.

As long as we had available credit, which we had tons of, and as long as we made our payments on time, which we always did, we were on top of things. We were good at keeping our heads above water. We looked great on paper. Gradually, though, a larger percentage of income went to satisfying minimum payments, and so a correspondingly larger share of our normal monthly living expenses was put on credit. We sometimes used cheaper credit to pay off more expensive credit. I know: craziness. We thought we had a handle on it.

Then came the disasters of economic recession and a massive credit crunch, and our cards' limits were abruptly lowered to their actual balances. At the same time, both of our paychecks shrank due to state furlough days. Less money came in. The same or more had to go out. And we had no more room on our plastic to smooth over the difference. We briefly considered declaring bankruptcy but decided against it. These debts were morally ours. It was only fair that we repay them.

Now we give a sizable chunk of change every month to pay down our defunct cards, and for everything else, we live on cash. We have no safety net. It's unsettling. There is a certain purity in going to the grocery store with a small, finite amount of cash and buying only the bare necessities. But I often feel wistful for the days when I bought whatever I thought might make my family happy. I am reminded of the old commercial for the state lottery, where a guy who just won millions is browsing the dairy aisle of the grocery store, and the hipster voiceover of epiphany says something like, "Wow, like, I could totally afford all this *cheese*." When I am shopping now, I feel the opposite. I totally can't afford any cheese.

There are things I no longer do under the New Austerity. I no longer renew magazine subscriptions, go to the movies, or send flowers. I no longer pay for a car wash or pick up a pizza, treat myself to Starbucks, or drop clothes at the dry cleaner. I no longer participate in the school fundraisers of my coworkers' children, give money to charity, or buy Tupperware/Avon/Pampered Chef or any other products that support the friends who sell them. You'd think by now the empty pockets of someone who used to be such a profligate spender would be noticeably affecting the local economy.

The withdrawal symptoms are easing, little by little. There are still tough moments as we battle our addiction one day at a time. For cheap therapy, we started a blog about our extreme budget, called "The Thinner Wallet," named by my husband for the condition of our wallets when we removed those thick stacks of charge cards. At first those wallets seemed flaccid, anemic, no longer full of possibility. But the thinner wallets we both now carry signify positivity, a healthy financial decision, a moving forward. With time and self-discipline, we will grow older, wiser, and solvent. In five years, we'll, like, totally be able to pay cash for all that cheese.

A Living Wage

(2017)

Women keep the Catholic Church going. That is my thesis. Visit any parish on any day, and you will mostly find women performing the daily work that must be done between Sundays. Women run the parish offices and religious education programs and other necessary ministries. They sit on the parish council and balance the books. Women often clean the pews and the restrooms and the rectories. Women are cantors and lectors and eucharistic ministers. The priests and deacons at the altar and in charge of sacraments are male in the Catholic tradition, but there are parishes administered by female lay pastoral associates. At street level, women are the hands and feet of Jesus.

Women historically have taught in the Catholic schools and ministered in the Catholic hospitals, but they were women religious, sisters who belonged to religious orders. They lived in community, and their material needs were scant. But in this new century, there are fewer nuns and more laywomen who are employed by the Church. While the Church relies on volunteers in many instances, certain jobs require steady commitment and extensive training, which must be compensated. It's a matter of economic justice.

My examples are anecdotal rather than statistical, but as a laywoman who once worked for the Church, I can attest that the problem of earning a living wage while doing God's work is real.

I was able to work part-time as a director of religious education for a medium-sized parish because my husband's health insurance covered our whole family, a circumstance that the Church too often counts on. If I had been single, I would not have taken that job. I couldn't have afforded it. My parish job, which the pastor offered me after I'd volunteered many hours for many years, provided a second (small) income for our family.

But single women and single mothers do work for the Church. The wages they earn, especially in urban areas, barely cover their living expenses. A friend who works full-time for the Church reports that after she pays rent and buys groceries and fills up the car with gas, nothing is left. Another woman moonlights at an all-night convenience store to make ends meet, this after a long day of ministry. A youth minister I know can't get a second job because her work schedule is so variable. She is responsible for retreats and field trips and sacramental prep along with the many extra hours she devotes to her beloved teens. She loves her work, but she is tired of having to move every time her rent is raised. Her budget is that tight.

Some parishes are now splitting the duties of paid positions, such as music ministry or religious education, between two part-time employees, thus sidestepping the obligation to provide their workers with benefits like health care and retirement. Not that these benefits, even when they are provided, are expansive. A friend who taught in a Catholic school for ten years reports that her retirement income from that job amounts to $232 a month. Is it any wonder she joined the secular workforce?

We can work for love, but we can't eat it.

As I talked with people about this fraught topic, I realized that my thesis was sexist. This dilemma is not the exclusive province of women. I know a wonderful man who had to leave a job he loved as a chaplain in detention ministry because he could not support his growing family on what he earned. Here is someone who passionately believes in restorative justice and wants to work with a population that many would shun, but he can't swing it financially. He had to find more lucrative work. He still volunteers in the jails when he can carve some time out of his job duties and his family time, but he is another example of the Church losing quality vocations due to not accounting for the practicalities of life.

Working for the Church is joyful and fulfilling and infuriating and really hard. It is also a calling. No one I know goes into Church work for the money, but that does not absolve the institutional Church of the responsibility to pay its lay workers a just wage. If the parish budget is actually its mission statement, the line items should reflect a commitment to paying employees fairly, to compensating them in a way that frees them to commit to their hearts' work while still being able to honor their financial obligations.

If the Church wants its people to heed God's call, the Church would do well to give its workers this day enough for their daily bread.

Addiction

Good Morning, My Beautiful Child
(2020)

A friend who had a baby several months before I had my first child told me that one of the best parts of becoming a parent is that it gives us a glimpse into the beginning of our own lives, the period of our infancy that we don't remember. As we diaper and feed our newborn, as we marvel and coo at this miraculous being, we get to see how our parents once marveled and cooed over us. We new parents, instantly on the other side of unconditional love, are granted insight into the parents who gave us life. And we suddenly get how our parents can still love us with such holy ferocity even though we have grown up and messed up and disappointed them and maybe even broken their hearts.

I remembered the power of that realization when I read the message that former Vice President and now Democratic presidential candidate Joe Biden allegedly wrote to his son Hunter while Hunter was in rehab for drug addiction. Hunter had texted an apology to his dad for being a "f*cked-up addict" and for possibly damaging his father's political aspirations. "Good morning, my beautiful son," Joe Biden wrote back, "I miss you and love you. Dad."

So much about this simple exchange of text messages flooded my heart with an overflow of emotion and empathy. First, that the elder Biden signed his message, as though Hunter couldn't see who it was from, because my kids always find it hilarious and old-school when I sign a message or identify myself in a voicemail. "We know who you are, Mom," they say with fond exasperation.

Second, as the parent of a child who has battled the kind of addiction that led to some very "f*cked-up" situations, I suspect that this text may have been Hunter's attempt to make a very big amends to his father, because making amends is an essential part of any 12-step program of recovery. And his father gave the perfect reply to a child who is sorry and shaky and demoralized and has no idea how to fix the damage caused: the recommitment to unconditional love.

A parent of an addict believes fervently in the God of Second Chances. We pray to the God of Second Chances, that our child will not be found dead, that our child will know that the door home is always open, that our child will find a way out of pain and peril to health and happiness. We pray for a helpful stranger to reach out to our child, because we know any path to healing will not be through us, even though we would do anything for that child. We wait, like the father of the Prodigal Son in the Gospel. We too watch and hope for our child to appear on the horizon. Sometimes our son or daughter does come home, dirty and sick, out of options, having landed at the bottom-most bottom of their addiction. Sometimes we get the phone call: Come pay the bail bond. Or come claim the body. Sometimes we just never hear.

So many family members, not just parents, know the worry and torment of loving an addict. When I first read Joe Biden's message, I imagined I was not alone in descending into the deep well of this all-too-common experience. I know that pain and that love. It seemed to me that the opposing presidential candidate would use that pain and that love as weapons of ridicule at his own peril: the love of a parent for a child who looks like a failure to society cries out to all parents who continue to love and pray for their children no matter their f*ck-ups or flaws. A parent's compassion for a suffering child is fully operational from the moment of the child's birth, from cradle to dreaded grave and even beyond, summoned by ancient strands of DNA and the sacred urge to nurture this beautiful and beloved life.

And third, the sweet message to "my beautiful son" resonates with every parent who has paid the bail, who has provided access to rehab, who has helped clean up the past wreckage of a child who is committed to recovery. Recovery from addiction is a personal endeavor, an ongoing process, a journey rather than a destination: "One day at a time" and all that. You know as a parent that you can't do the work for your child, even though you wish you could. You would give your own life gladly to save your child. But you can't coerce the commitment to clean living. You can't force the Twelve Steps on anyone who is not willing to take the first step. You are powerless, except for prayer. But in the midst of praying to the God of Second (or Third or Fourth) Chances, you can take a moment to send the text message about loving and missing your beautiful child, the child you have loved from birth, the child who has gladdened your days, the child who has broken your heart but will always own your heart.

Rather than blame or chastise, Joe Biden, who already knows the immeasurable grief of losing a child, told his son that he was more important than a campaign, than a reputation, than an election, than *anything*. Joe Biden's text made me remember all the hard times with my daughter, and all the progress she has made, and how grateful I am for her life, and how proud I am of her. I imagine a cosmic union of hearts with all the other parents who are similarly moved. I tell you, for us, that text from a father is the essence of God's grace.

The Other Deadly Plague

(2020)

Since 1999, more than 450,000 Americans have died as a result of opioid use. My beautiful 20-year-old niece was one of them. Our family is one in a statistic of grief.

If you know anyone who is hooked on opioids, you know the heartache. You know the desperation of trying to find help for your loved ones, of trying to stick with them through recovery and relapse, of trying to salvage all the lives left in ruins. You may also know about mourning the deceased.

The millions of Americans dependent on or addicted to opioids straddle all lines of age, gender, race, creed, and socio-economic status. Maybe they needed relief from the ongoing pain of a work-related injury, or maybe they needed help to manage temporary discomfort after surgery, or maybe they needed to escape the agony of a chronic medical condition. The power of opioids saved them. They were pain-free. Then they were dependent on that daily dose. Then they had to up the dose. Then they were addicted. Then, if they could no longer wangle a prescription or couldn't afford their supply, they sometimes turned to heroin or fentanyl to avoid or ease their withdrawal symptoms. And all along, a public health crisis grew.

The number of American fatalities is staggering, but even harder to fathom is that each death represents a family and a community deprived of a beloved member. There is a web of loss connected to each curtailed life, to each wasted potential, to each journey of suffering. The enormity of our collective grief is magnified by each death.

How does a family heal from such tragedy? My own heart has been hacked in half by my niece's death, which was ruled an accidental fentanyl overdose. She is a bright candle snuffed out far too soon. I've watched her parents and her siblings deal with this unthinkable loss. The well of mourning seems bottomless. The saddest sight I've ever seen in my life was my brother and sister-in-law exiting the funeral home where their daughter's body had been cremated. My sister-in-law held the huge spray of pink roses that had rested on her daughter's coffin. My brother held a small-handled bag containing the urn with his daughter's ashes. Their bodies seemed to struggle to remain standing, to stay upright, to keep from crumbling. Their grief was heavier than gravity.

"The LORD is close to the brokenhearted," says the psalmist (Ps 34:19). The Lord must be very busy these days.

What do we do, what can we do, how do we save our families, our communities, from this deadly scourge? I wish I knew the answers to these huge questions. Education is a start. Treatment options instead of prison is another approach. Taking legal action, some people are slowly calling to account the corporations—and the moneymakers hiding behind them—who cynically hawked these addictive drugs, who valued profit over human life, who are responsible for so much devastation. But all the compensatory fines in the world will not bring back the life of a son or daughter, a mother or father, a spouse or sibling. The epidemic of addiction is all around us. It enfolds and ensnares us. It calls for creative solutions and nonstop prayer before it swallows our society whole.

Crises of Faith

Sunday Crybaby

(2017)

Sunday Mass is in my DNA. This wasn't always a given. For a brief time, mostly during my high school and undergrad years, I did not go to Mass. I rebelled. I flirted with atheism. What I saw in the Church was at worst hypocrisy, at best rote boredom. When I got my driver's license, my mother thought I was taking my younger sister to Mass. We usually went to the park instead, only stopping by the church to snag a dated bulletin to offer as evidence.

Before I flew to Europe to spend a college semester in Rome, my mother made me go to confession, in case the plane crashed. With the brashness of youth, I told the priest that I was there under duress, and that I couldn't think of anything I wanted to share with him. He was wise enough to have a conversation with me about the gift of travel rather than try to convert me.

A semester in Europe with a Eurail pass meant that I immersed myself in history. I visited churches and chapels and cathedrals. I walked through the piazza in front of the Vatican almost daily. I marveled at the Sistine Chapel. I took a tour of Chartres. I went to an organ recital in Notre Dame. But I never once, in the midst of all that Catholicism, went to Mass. I regret that now. At the time, I thought it wasn't for me.

Mass found me in my senior year of college at a Catholic university, and I've been going back ever since. I finally got it: the ritual, the communal celebration, the Eucharist, the palpable presence of God. I haven't always been purely concentrated on worship. While my children were growing up, I often was more concerned that they behave in church than I was in tune with the Mass. I worked at a parish for eight years, and often had to orchestrate the participation of students in Children or Youth Masses. I loved Mass, but it was part of my job. I was a go-to person in church, always busy, never still.

Now, however, I usually go to Mass alone. I am anonymous in many different parishes, as there is not one I call home right now. I usually sit in a pew that I think of as "All the Single Ladies," as we seek each other out and make room for each other without exchanging a word. I think we spot each other by the secret signal of fanning ourselves with the bulletin, even in cold weather.

And each Sunday, I usually find myself in tears at some point before the final blessing.

You might say it's hormonal. Or the deep satisfying breath that is only taken when one is at rest in a pew, where there is time to think, to reflect, to slow down, to let go. Or the reverence that Mass instills in me. Maybe it's all of the above. But there is something every Sunday that so deeply touches my nomadic Catholic soul that my eyes fill with tears. Sometimes I choke up. It may be a choir that is so full of joy that their music makes me cry. It may be the incense rising in a holy cloud as we in the pews are blessed. It may be an Irish hymn that reminds me of my mother, who died this past year. It may be a family of hopeful faces, whose three young children are baptized during the Mass. Or last week: a little boy who had lost his father that very week led us in the Our Father, his voice sweet and clear. How could these things not make me cry?

I imagine I look like the odd old bird, sniffling during the homily, blowing her nose at the offertory, or turning a tear-stained beak to wish a stranger peace. It's fine. I am a Sunday crybaby, the lady my own children would have felt sorry for, the crone who must have experienced some terrible sadness to make her weep so openly. But I am usually not sad. I am just moved to witness the Spirit so alive and so well. I am an open heart, so grateful to be so loved by God. I might have come in wounded, but during Mass I am healed and made whole by the risen Jesus, who accepts me as I am and sends me back out there for the week.

It turns out I am not alone in being a Sunday crybaby. A few months ago, I went to Mass with my brother-in-law. The communion song was "Be Not Afraid," and as usual, I had to stop singing at the point when the song overwhelmed me and I could no longer get out the words. Then I noticed: he had stopped singing. There was a tear on his cheek, too. "That song gets me," he said, a bit embarrassed. I just smiled. I know, brother. I know.

Emangelization, or the Stone Age of Spirituality

(2015)

The serendipity of the internet works like this: you read an article, which links to a definition, which links to an essay, which links to a website, and before you know it, you are visiting a virtual space that you would never have discovered on your own. That was how I landed at an interview conducted by the New Emangelization Project.

I know: that word is giving my spell-check heart failure. But I have transcribed it correctly. "Emangelization" is the word created by those who believe that the Catholic Church is threatened by modern gender issues and needs to get back to its masculine roots immediately. The goal of the project, then, is to evangelize men, or to "emangelize."

A Catholic woman cannot be faulted for the double take she does upon reading, in the words of a prominent American cardinal, that the Church has become "very feminized." The Catholic Church, that most patriarchal of religious institutions, where it is considered sinful even to discuss the ordination of women, where some parishes ban girls from being altar servers, where the men's groups are "Knights" and the women's are "Daughters"? My double take was practically a triple take.

Since the discovery of the New Emangelization, this essay's rewriting has gone through the five stages of grief, from denial to anger to bargaining to depression to acceptance. OK, perhaps not ending in acceptance, but I have tossed earlier versions that were mad or sad or mocking, because the issue of inclusion deserves to be treated with serious respect. The misconception at the heart of the New Emangelization is one that plagues many civic and religious entities throughout the world; that is, that women and men are fighting a war that must produce a clear winner and a clear loser. For the Church, this thinking represents a giant step backwards.

Along with the physical evolution of species, the human race is also in the process of spiritual evolution, which can be traced through recorded time. The evolution of the spirit has brought us to a place in history where we have outlawed slave owner-ship, we aspire not to discriminate against any group or indi-vidual that is different from ourselves, and we attempt to honor the human dignity of each person in our global village. This evolution has also confronted issues of gender, and women in the western world have risen from the status of property to one of at least political equality. This is not so in other parts of the world, where women are still bought and sold, enslaved and downtrodden, assaulted and victimized, and denied education and other basic rights. The New Emangelization, then, in seek-ing to prioritize and elevate men over women in the name of traditional religion, is a detour from spiritual evolution. It is a weak cousin of the Taliban or ISIS or Boko Haram, organiza-tions that aggressively oppress women as a matter of faith.

Am I overreacting? I cite biblical backup, Paul's letter to the Galatians, which states that in Christ "there is not male and female" (Gal 3:28). This is one goal of spiritual growth. Our earthly gender, or "all of this nonsense of sexual confusion," in the good cardinal's estimation, is a non-issue in the realm of God. To state that men will return to the practice of Ca-tholicism, or be emangelized, when the Church reinstates "a certain manly discipline" or "the man-like character of devo-tion and sacrifice" or "the powerful manliness of the Mass" would be ridiculous if it were not so dangerously seductive to some folks. To put forth that *manly is good* and *womanly is bad* is not only dismissive of half the world's population, it is a disservice to all of us, as well as to the gospel message.

"Women are wonderful, of course," says the cardinal patronizingly, and rather disingenuously, after citing all the ways that women and their radical feminism have been the ruin of good Catholic men. We women *are* wonderful. And so are men. We are each of us wondrously made and called equally to be about the work of God, an evangelization that knows no gender, in spite of those who would divide and conquer in God's name.

The Theme of Change Remains the Same

(2015)

The stories of the Bible often serve as proof that no matter how many thousands of years pass, our fundamental human distaste for change has endured. We humans don't like change. This struck me anew while I was reading a daily passage from the Hebrew Scriptures. The Israelites had been subjugated and enslaved in Egypt until Moses, God's agent of change, orchestrated their release from captivity. But God's chosen people, who so gratefully followed Moses out of their bondage in Egypt, were unprepared for the desert that followed. "The people grumbled against Moses," the book of Exodus tells us, "saying, 'Why then did you bring us up out of Egypt? To have us die of thirst with our children and our livestock?'" (Exod 17:3) At that moment they preferred slavery to the uncertainty of change. The story is a perfect example of the Irish proverb: "Better the devil you know than the devil you don't."

Change jangles us. We like to feel comfortable and in control of our lives. We sometimes get so comfortable that we believe nothing will ever change. When change does happen, sometimes imposed on us by events we cannot dictate, we rebel. We want stasis. In the midst of upheaval, we often question, as the bumper sticker asks, "Where are we going, and why are we in this handbasket?" We make dire predictions about the outcome of an unexpected change. We are prepared for every change to be for the worse.

But God is a God of change. The world of God's creation is in constant flux. Change is all we have; ironically, it is the one constant of our physical lives. The life God gives us is a litany of changes. From the moment we exist, our bodies begin the process of change. We parents measure the ounces and inches our babies gain, and we delight in each new milestone: first rollover, first tooth, first word, and on through the years of firsts, kindergarten and soccer trophies, report cards and menstruation, braces and heartbreaks, driver's licenses and graduations, disappointments and triumphs, and all of the time between changes. As the seasons change, so do we. Our skeletons change, our looks change, our opinions change, our priorities change, our relationships change, our jobs change, our families change, our goals change. It makes me laugh when menopause is referred to as "the change," as though it is the change to end all changes. It is not. The changes that begin with birth end only with death. In between, however, are change and challenge, God and grace, light and love, all better known as life.

We learn along our earthly journey that any encounter with God is supposed to change us. When people in the Bible meet Jesus, they are profoundly changed. Fishermen leave their nets, tax collectors leave their bookkeeping, the wealthy part with their riches. The lame walk, the dead regain breath, the blind suddenly see. "Were not our hearts burning within us?" ask the disciples who met Jesus on the road to Emmaus (Luke 24:32). They know that they will never be the same after that holy walk. They have experienced *metanoia*, the radical change of heart that happens when we give ourselves over to God's will rather than our own. We too are called to leave our former, unenlightened ways. When we open ourselves to God, we should know that change is inevitable. It may be uncomfortable. It may chafe. It may hurt. It may be the hardest thing we've ever done.

But if we are mindful of the presence of God in our lives, we try to go gracefully with the changes. Resistant at first, we learn to let go. We bend, we adapt, we are converted. We find peace only when we stop struggling against change and instead look for God right there in the midst of it. Because God, who loves to see us change, is there.

A Dry Spell

(2019)

Mental flashbacks to 2002 have plagued my brain lately. That was the year, dramatized in the movie *Spotlight*, when a series of *Boston Globe* articles exposed the scandal of the clergy's sexual abuse of children in the local Catholic Church. In 2002 I worked for the Church across the country in California, and just answering the phone in the parish office in the days and weeks and months of that explosive reporting was harrowing. Angry and betrayed people said terrible things, for which there was no defense.

These many years later, we still endure revelations of documented accusations and consequences—or the lack thereof—involving clergy members and the harm done to their victims, children and adults, males and females. And there is still no defense. Pope Francis called the world's bishops to a Vatican summit to address this ongoing crisis in the Church, to find ways to end the grinding cycle of criminal abuse and subsequent cover-up, but seemingly nothing proactive came of that meeting. A future task force is not what we were hoping for.

Now it's Lent again, a time of repentance and rebirth, both of which this Church of ours sorely needs. Both of which do not seem forthcoming.

And I just feel tired.

These truly horrible scandals are the work of the human Church, the hierarchical Church, but they affect the whole Church, the people of God. We're all tired. Friends and family members have left the Church, no longer able to abide the bad actors. The Church's reputation is in tatters, shredded by each new publication of a shameful history of abuse and cover-up in yet another diocese. With scattered exceptions, members of the clergy don't seem to understand the anger and desolation of the laypeople. I wouldn't be surprised if the Holy Spirit were also exhausted, what with trying to blow the gentle winds of renewal through the unyielding wall of the defenders of the structural Church.

I sense only fatigue in the wind right now.

During Lent we read in the Gospels about Jesus' time in the desert. Just after Jesus was baptized, the Holy Spirit led him to the desert, where he ate nothing for 40 days and nights and was tempted by the devil himself. Jesus must have been awfully tired from all that. Perhaps right now we are in the desert, too, at least metaphorically. I know I am. I am stumbling on tumble-weeds in a vast baked and bleak expanse. I am in a dry spell.

My soul feels parched. I know there is water in the well, but it seems like a lot of work to get to it. I am drifting through a lethargic Lent. A sentiment I spotted online recently was something like, "For Lent, I'm giving up." Those of us in the desert can relate.

With effort, I remind myself that it's easy to lose sight of the things that don't get any press. For example, there is so much good that is done by so many unsung holy people of the Church. There are those who truly go about doing God's work every day among us, who feed the hungry and shelter the homeless and care for the sick and visit the imprisoned and fight for justice. I am in awe of the faithful folks who keep on spreading the works of mercy even in the shadow of scandal and sorrow. I am heartened by their labor. I am inspired by their steadfast commitment to love.

Jesus returns from the desert, Luke tells us, "in the power of the Spirit" (Luke 4:14). He then begins his fateful public ministry. As I reflect on Jesus emerging from that exhausting ordeal, rolling up his holy sleeves, and getting down to work, I see that I too need to focus on the things that I can do, on the things I am called to do. I may be fed up with the Church's hierarchy, and I sure can't fix anything happening high above my head, but I can find some small measure of water. More importantly, I can give water to the thirsty. It occurs to me that my faith requires nothing less than this.

Fall Down; Lift Up; Repeat

(2019)

While I was out of state over the Christmas holiday, I went to Mass at a parish not my own. The thing about Mass somewhere new is that even though the building and the pre-sider and the music and the liturgical details and the people around you are completely unknown to you, the Mass is the Mass, and that is comforting. You are home spiritually even though you aren't home geographically. I've said this before, but I felt it anew: I love going to Mass somewhere else. It's like a refresher course for faith.

The pastor of the church I visited mentioned in his homily, and I repeat it with gratitude, that one thing he had learned in all his years on this earth was that if he fell down, as inevitably we all do, he knew that God would lift him up. Heads around me nodded. They were mostly older heads. We could all think of times we had fallen down, in failure, in despondency, in grief, in the soul's desert, in anger, in sin. Yet we were all at Mass on this windy morning. At some point in our lives, we had all experienced being lifted up. And this grace had been given to us more than once.

I looked around the church. As is common in Catholic churches, the images of the Stations of the Cross wound their way around the walls, depicting from one to fourteen the heart-wrenching journey of Good Friday. As I thought about the homily, I realized that three of the stations show Jesus falling down. After the first two falls, Jesus is lifted up by people who love him: his mother Mary, a compassionate Veronica who wipes his face, and the women of Jerusalem. After the third fall, Jesus is crucified. Then he dies, the ultimate fall. Again, the people who love him are present, and lay him in his tomb. He falls down; he is lifted up. On Easter Jesus is lifted back to life in the mystery of the resurrection. Forty days later, he is literally lifted up in the ascension. The times Jesus falls and is subsequently lifted up are part of his human story. Jesus as brother has been one of us; he has dwelt among us.

The cycle of falling down and being lifted up is the story of humanity. Our own experiences are usually not as spectacular or as horrific as the life of Jesus, but we know where he has been. We have been there, too. Whether we fall short or fall down, we know what it's like to find ourselves on the ground, flat on our faces. Everything is wrong. We have failed; we have messed up; we have burnt out. And then, whether we call it God or grit, we are lifted up, set back up on our own two feet, a little wiser, a little more resilient.

Often God lifts us up through the help of others, as we see in the simple gesture of mercy between Veronica and Jesus. It may be our loved ones who care deeply about us, or it may be a stranger. We fall down, and someone reaches out to us. It may take a few tries, but in the end, we are lifted up. If we look carefully, we will see the face of God.

Philosophers and skeptics have long debated the methods for proving or disproving the existence of God. Syllogisms and treatises fill scholarly books. To my simple mind, there is a simple answer, found in the First Letter of John: "God is love" (4:8). Love definitely exists. To borrow a phrase, the proof of God's pudding is in the loving. In my life I have found that what lifts me up is love. Wherever I see love, I see God. Whenever I give love, I feel God. However I know love, I sense God. That's all the proof I can expect. Sometimes, it is enough to lift me up.

Romance/Mixed-Faith Marriage

Making Other Plans

(2004)

My daughter is dating a Baptist.

Well, she says, he's not really a Baptist. He was baptized something Protestant, and he attends a church that happens to be Baptist. But he is, vehemently, non-Catholic.

My daughter is in her twenties, self-supporting, a woman on the verge of everything. She has adopted San Diego as her home. Her boyfriend is soft-spoken, attractive, kind. He is from the Midwest, and we try not to make fun of his slight Fargo accent. Being Californians, we think we have no accent. Until one ventures from home, no one has an accent.

But I digress. The point is that my daughter's nice, transplanted boyfriend is not Catholic.

A childhood chant came back to me recently—not a holy one, but one from the church of outdoor games. During the long evenings of summer, we played hide-and-seek in the fading light, our innocuous hiding places becoming more ominous as they were enrobed in darkness. The person who was "it" chanted as a courtesy to those who were too slow-witted or nervous to have found a hiding place by the count of fifty:

"Apples, peaches, pumpkin pie! Who's not ready? Holler 'I'!" Hardly any of us ever hollered. A holler, revealing location, was an act of desperation.

I'm hollering now, Lord. That's me, hollering. I'm not ready.

I'm not ready to be the mother of adult children. Just when I thought I would always haul a diaper bag and a car seat everywhere I went, I found myself teaching teenagers how to drive. Just when I thought I would always tuck little ones in with bedtime stories and then feel small bodies in the wee hours slipping into my bed, I found myself dropping children off at college dorms and renting apartments in other cities. In recent photographs, I am the one next to the vibrant and beautiful young person. I am the one who looks like somebody's mother. It happened as quickly as I was told it would.

But back to my daughter's sort-of-Baptist boyfriend. He looks so good to a mother who wants perfect men for her daughters. He actually goes to a Bible study class, rarely drinks, goes to school, drives a safe car, lives in his own apartment, and has a steady job. I know she wants to keep him. My problem is that I secretly want to convert him.

Before he converts her.

On the phone she told me that she had gone to his church that Sunday instead of going to Mass. I could hear my voice go up an octave, even though I tried to stop it, as I said, "Oh?"

"It was great," she said. "All we did was sing songs and listen to the sermon. We didn't have to do all that stand-up-and-kneel-down, over-and-over, boring Catholic stuff."

"You mean like the Eucharist?" I asked, more acidly than I intended.

"I knew I shouldn't talk to you about this," she said. "Mom, this was *interesting*!"

Twelve years of religious education, and my daughter is no defender of the faith.

I want to blame myself: first, as the mother, who should have done more holy things around the house, who should have lit a hotter Catholic home fire; and second, as the parish director of religious education where she attended her confirmation classes, who should have held on tighter to post-confirmation students, who should have inspired a deeper hunger for the Eucharist, who should have at least recruited more exciting musicians. She has slipped away.

My friends and I now have kids who are coming out of closets, going into depressions, giving birth in and out of wedlock, breaking hearts and mending broken ones, traveling to New Zealand, studying their brains out, dropping out of school, joining the Peace Corps, going to war. We are none of us ready. But ready or not, here they come. They need love and advice and loans and help with car insurance. They move away, come home, move again, come back to visit. They amaze us with their resilience and flexibility and optimism. Their futures stretch farther than they can see, and they take another day and another chance for granted. They really think they will someday find what they want to be when they grow up, and have no idea that today, this day, is the day that they already are grown up. They don't see the ladder formed by choices they have already made. Life is what happens in spite of our plans.

When I had those babies long ago, I thought being a mother meant I was in charge. I thought those babies would always look up to me and adore me and agree with me, even as I encouraged them to be independent thinkers. Which is what they have become. On some days I think that things have really gotten away from me.

On other days I know that I am planted where I am meant to be.

At least, says my husband, our daughter has a relationship with God, a God she loves and worships and seeks to serve, even if she does so in a non-Catholic way. Of course he is right. Of course we will always be hugely blessed in being her parents. She is an adult, and her spiritual decisions are hers alone, even if I still pray that someday God will guide her home. I'm imagining that someday we may see a Baptist wedding, and little Baptist grandchildren, and that will be OK. We will turn our search engines onto "ecumenism" and go through new doors.

I realize anew that, in this challenging game of life, God is always "It." We can pretend that we are "it," but we are not. "Ready or not, here I come!" says God, and we can only have faith that, as imperfect, hollering hiders, we will indeed be found. Again and again.

40 Shades of Gray

(2020)

The number 40 in the Bible is used to signify a really long time before something important happens: 40 days and nights of unrelenting rain for Noah keeping the faith in his ark, 40 years of wandering for God's chosen people before they get to the Promised Land, 40 days of fasting for Jesus in the desert. I am especially aware of this big number today, because it is our 40th wedding anniversary. I am not suggesting that anything important is about to happen, but it does feel like a really long time. In a good way.

I remember going to a party for my grandparents' 40th anniversary. They were very old, and a lot of old people had gathered to wish them well. I remember Great Aunt Sue look-ing like a toad and my brother saying under his breath, "Rib-bit." Forty years was obviously a ridiculously long time to be alive, let alone to be married.

And here we are. Me and this guy.

Isn't it one of the ironic parts of aging that we find ourselves at the advanced stages of life where we thought we'd be totally different when we reached them, but we are not? Today I in-habit my grandmother's skin, wondering how I got here, just as I now realize she must have felt the same way. It was 40 years ago today that I stood at the altar in my ecru wedding gown with the blue ribbon and promised this handsome young man in his formal morning coat that I'd stick with him through all those unimaginable opposites: better or worse, rich or poor, healthy or sick. He promised the same things.

And here we are. This guy and me. We've experienced all of those extremes together, and then some.

We can't complain about this life we've shared. We've raised four fantastic people. We've added a daughter-in-law, a son-in-law, a fiancé, and three grandchildren, all of them fantastic as well. We are reasonably healthy. We are recently retired. We still like each other. We still love each other. We still do the things that people in love do. So as not to mortify my chil-dren—"MOM!"—I'll stop there.

But, man, 40 is a huge number. It seems far more ominous and possibly terminal than 39. Maybe it's the Age of COVID we're living in that makes me ponder how much longer we may have together on God's green earth. We could be looking at another 20 or 30 years of marriage, but the odds surely worsen as the years pile up.

Morbid, I know. But we can hardly deny the cycles of life.

My grandmother was at my wedding, possibly remembering the vows she'd made so many decades ago. She was habitually irritated with my grandfather until the day he died, whereupon he became a saint. Marriage was different in those days: I know she never thought of herself as a full partner in anything they did or decided to do. Wives were subservient and compliant and often secretly resentful. Marriage, thank our lucky stars, has come a long way.

And here we are. This guy and I have decisions ahead, as well as curves and forks in the road that we can't anticipate. But I wouldn't want to be traveling it with anyone else. My husband is kind and smart and funny and supportive and romantic. Sometimes he worries too much, but sometimes so do I. Our marriage has a rhythm that I can only attribute to God's grace, because we have bad days on different days. One of us is strong when the other is weak. One of us is hopeful when the other is despondent. One of us is unwavering when the other is full of doubt. One of us is cheerful when the other is blue. One of us is balanced when the other is too close to the edge. We've managed this marriage for 40 years. I think it's going to last.

Our first kiss happened on September 13, 1978, when we were in college. We got married two years later on the same date because it was a Saturday. On this September 13, the world is a completely different proposition. Many of our loved ones are gone, our bones creak and we say "What?" a lot, we cannot gather with family or have a party, but all is well. We'll look through our wedding album and Zoom with our family and watch the sunset and immerse ourselves in blessed gratitude.

Because here we are.

The Marriage Couple

(2021)

Oh, hey, it's the marriage couple!"

That comment was directed at us. I waved back. My husband and I had just given a workshop on Catholic marriage at a Ministry Conference in Texas. It was our first presentation and, as it turned out, our last.

I thrilled to that moment of recognition. I envisioned a future wherein we were The Marriage Couple, recognizable, in demand for conferences nationwide, making our living on the Catholic speaker circuit. My first book, a collection of essays on marriage and intimacy, was on sale in the vendors' area. We gave our workshop twice to small groups. The second time was better.

At Mass that evening, however, something was in the air. Something was changing. The husband of The Marriage Couple didn't go to Communion.

The husband, at long last, was done being Catholic.

I knew my husband was struggling with the faith we'd always shared. The sex abuse crisis hit him hard, being as he was an elementary school teacher and a tireless advocate for children. The attempted cover-ups of the molestation and violence that had been perpetrated on children were just as terrible. The Church's seeming lack of love for LGBTQ+ people, one of whom was our adult child, left a bitter taste. Our child wanted nothing to do with the Church that had rejected them. Then an angry deacon told my husband that the Eucharist was all the reason one needed to be Catholic, and something in my husband's heart broke free. It wasn't enough for him. He may have had other reasons. No matter what they were, I know he was following his conscience. He left the Church.

Just as we'd become The Marriage Couple.

The blow to my ego was painful, but it was nothing compared to the reality of a faith no longer shared. Our kids long grown, I went to Mass alone. I thought about the way we always used to keep holding hands after the Our Father, up until our hug at the Sign of Peace, and I yearned for that. When I saw other couples together at Mass, I missed the solid presence of my husband next to me, the sound of him, the smell of him. It had never occurred to me that we wouldn't become one of the ancient couples at Mass. I felt like a Mass widow.

My husband stopped going into the prison with me on Saturdays to facilitate Catholic communion services. It was a ministry we'd both loved, but he no longer heard the call. I partnered instead with other volunteers. Arriving early one morning, I knelt by the tabernacle in the prison chapel and prayed for my marriage: not the legality of it, but the sacrament of it. I mourned the loss of the holiness of our union, which sounds silly now. I was just so sad. In that simple space, in my heart, I heard a calm voice: "You are married to *me*."

What? I thought. Something in me lurched. And then comfort flooded through my being. My earthly marriage was an important and beautiful thing, but it was not *the* thing. Those five words brought me peace. I knew I loved my husband and would happily live out my days with him. I knew our marriage was sacred, because we treated it that way. But I also knew in that moment that my essence, my non-temporal self, my soul, belonged only to God.

That was a decade ago. I still miss my husband at Mass. I miss the shared practice of our faith. But I let go of my concern with appearances. I said goodbye to the dream of The Marriage Couple. Now we're just a married couple—imperfect, holy, normal—who love and cherish each other and accept each other as we are: Thanks be to God.

Raising Children

Sugar and Spice and Everything Pierced

(2003)

You may want to nominate me for Worst-Mother-of-the-Year, but my daughters got pierced for Christmas. And I don't mean their earlobes. I mean we took a trip to the local tattoo parlor, where the artist Spike (not his real name) accepts cash only, and where the price list displays a head-spinning array of body part options for piercing. When we left, my college freshman had a hoop through her nostril, and my high school freshman sported one just above her navel. This is called body jewelry. This is also the point at which I am tempted to begin every sentence with, "When I was your age . . ."

The thing is, I am not their age. They didn't know me when I wore patched jeans and secondhand vests and my hair reached to my belt. Not that I wore a belt, because belts were in a very uncool phase. They didn't know me when I went braless and didn't shave my legs to show solidarity with the emerging feminist movement, much to the consternation of my own parents.

But these are secrets from my past that I would do well to keep in mind as I see my daughters through their own phases of heavy gothic makeup, zigzag parts in their hair, tiny shirts, and now piercings. They are at the age when we try on different looks, manners of speech and movement, philosophies, and personalities. With adolescence comes the realization that we are not our folks, and that we don't have to be our folks, thank the Lord. We experiment with our inner beings and our public masks. We begin to identify our unique gifts and shortcomings. We imitate those we admire. We become our adult selves, one revelation at a time.

As mothers, we are taken aback when our darlings dare to be different from us, when they spend too much time on makeup, or hate to read, or vote Republican. They become young adults, growing in grace and self-assurance, and we are so proud of them. At the same time, they reject things dear to our hearts, and we feel mystified and hurt. Mothering is surely a double-edged sword. Sometimes the apple seems to fall miles from the tree. Sometimes the apple seems to be taken up into the vortex of a tornado and thrown violently to the other side of the world. If children were apples.

Because who are these be-hooped girls, sitting in my living room looking like refugees from a National Geographic special on ceremonial jewelry? One wears a thrift-shop full slip over many layers of clothing. One's hair leaps from her head in small, twisted flips. They are from the tribe of the future. But they are mine.

My husband and I had misgivings about these exotic Christmas gifts. But these are kids who do well in school, who volunteer to feed the hungry, who are kind to their family, and who are good friends. They have passionate senses of justice, as well as keen senses of humor. In short, they are as great as any teenagers could be. These oddly placed hoops that Spike says to wash twice a day with antibacterial soap will not change that. Perhaps our misgivings center more on what we fear our friends will think of us when they see our pierced lovelies. Which reminds us that even as fully formed adults, we must strive to be better and deeper people.

We joke with our kids that their children will find new and unthinkable ways to horrify them when they are the parents. "No fair!" their sweet darlings will say, "Why can't I get a horn implanted? Why can't I get antlers like Chelsea? Everyone at school has a third eye!" We try to think of things more terrible than tattoos and brandings, but surely the future will be stranger than our aging imaginations can conjure.

For now, we'll roll with their trends and searches for meaning, and hope to see their true natures emerging ever more strongly from their experiments.

The Nest, Empty

(2010)

My youngest of four children has moved out of the house. She is now sharing an apartment with one of her sorority sisters, a mere 50 miles from home. She is halfway through her freshman year of college. She is lovely, witty, compassionate, intelligent, thoughtful, and completely ready to be out of the nest. Just as her three siblings were before her.

I should be congratulating myself on a job well done: four kids out in the world, finding their way, figuring out who they are and who they intend to be, navigating the waters of adulthood. Instead, I am rattling around in her nearly empty bedroom, feeling sad and sorry for myself. It's really over. The years that sometimes seemed to drag have flown. My little birds have all fledged.

It's been, after all, almost three decades that I've had at least one child at home. Those children have been my life's work. No matter how good a job I do at work, no matter how many published credits I accumulate, my kids will always be my chef d'oeuvre, my magnum opus. They are my joy and my bequest. They are proof of God's existence and benevolence. They are the grace of God personified.

So: a mere melancholy mood. It is right and natural that children grow up and move out, that they branch out and blossom and bloom. As our children mature, the relationship between my husband and me also enters metamorphosis. We can luxuriate in the presence of each other. We can live by a more forgiving clock. We can focus on what it means to be just us.

Our fledglings flown, we remain in the nest. We'll be here. We'll still be good for the occasional loan, word of advice, laundry facilities, square meal, place to regroup, and holiday destination. The sheer physicality of parenting, the mess and immediacy of it, is over—I no longer know what every child is doing at every moment—but the spirituality of parenting endures.

Every time one of my little birds moves out, I suffer through a small mourning period. It's nothing like death, but I grieve for a simple time that will not return. This last flight out just seems so final. I look at the stray things she has left behind—high school yearbooks, a random beanie, a half-burnt candle—and indulge in a bit of a cry. And then I blow my nose and give myself a talking-to, to be just so grateful for the impossibly, deliriously blessed life God has lavished on me.

WWJD

(2009)

One of my daughter's friends marked the summer after her high school graduation by getting an abortion. She was petrified that her father would have her slightly older boyfriend thrown in jail, that she would have to put off going to college, and that her mother would disown her. My daughter tried to reason with her, telling her that she might someday regret throwing away this tiny life, urging her to tell her mom, suggesting to her that in less than nine months she could bless some childless couple with this baby. But the only solution her friend could see out of her predicament was to get rid of the pregnancy. She did not think of her missed period as a growing baby with a soul. She saw only doom in the plus sign on the stick of the pregnancy test.

The boyfriend, the baby-daddy, drove her to the clinic, 50 miles away. The abortion done, he dropped her at her sister's, where she stayed overnight. The boyfriend was also planning to go away to college soon. After promising the young woman carrying his child that their relationship would be better than ever as soon as they took care of this little misstep, he dropped out of the picture. I imagine him, like the cartoon coyote, hiding around the corner, out of breath, resting after running as fast as he could in the opposite direction from his close call, thanking his lucky stars.

When my daughter broke down and related this sad tale, I told her how touched I was by her courage, her clarity, and her conviction. I was sad that her friend had ended her pregnancy, but at the same time, I was glad for my daughter's response to her friend's quandary. I patted myself on the back for raising such a great kid.

And I have to admit that the next time I saw her friend, whom I have known since she was a little girl and whom I've always welcomed like one of my own, I treated her coolly. I couldn't help it. She knew that my daughter had told me what had happened, which she was not happy about, and which made her uncomfortable in our home. Feeling inhospitable but righteous, I made no effort to ease her mind.

Except that, while she was visiting with my daughter, she suddenly felt nauseous, and then feverish. She was sick to her stomach, and began to bleed again, after her bleeding had slowed the day before. As it had only been a week since the abortion, she was scared that something bad was happening. I heard my daughter telling her to call her sister. Her sister did not answer her phone. My daughter's friend told her that she had left the paperwork from the clinic, which explained all the aftercare instructions, in the former boyfriend's car. He also was not returning calls. It was 11:00 p.m. She was afraid the staff at the local emergency room would call her parents if she showed up there. She was in a panic. She didn't know what to do.

God help me, I thought it would teach this young woman a lesson to deal with this fallout by herself. I remained in another room while this crisis was unfolding, my point being: *Now how does it feel to have done what you did?*

Until I came to my senses. Good Lord, what was I doing? How could I sustain my mean-spirited inaction when this girl needed help? I looked up the number for the clinic in the yellow pages and had her call the 24-hour hotline. While she waited for the call back, I looked up her symptoms online and read the results to her. Since the abortion had taken place more than several days before, she was probably not in danger of hemorrhage or a perforated uterus, but more likely had just overdone it in trying to get back to her normal life. The call back from the hotline affirmed this. She needed to rest, and to come in for a follow-up appointment. We made her a cup of tea and put her to bed.

Later, I reflected on my behavior, and on my calling as a follower of Christ to do the right thing. I suspect that the practice of my faith does not lie in condemning a young woman who has done a bad thing. Rather, it lies in showing her compassion, and in demonstrating how to take care of the sorrowing, the suffering, the sinful, among whom we are all numbered. It occurs to me that that's what Jesus did.

Child of Mine

(2021)

I f you are the parent of a lesbian, gay, bisexual, transgender, or queer (LGBTQ+) child, you've learned this lesson: when a child comes out of the closet, parents have to come out, too. The first sign of love in the form of acceptance that you can give your precious child is to affirm and celebrate them. You may have plenty of questions, but your child needs to know that you are neither ashamed of them nor disappointed in them. They are counting on your love.

A gay friend told me, right after my child came out, that parents are the hardest of all to tell. He said that you fear their rejection more than anyone else's. That usually you put off telling them until last, until you really have no choice, because by now everyone else knows. My friend told me I should feel proud that my child felt safe to tell me before most others.

Still, this news can be a shock. When our children come out to us, we have to face the unconscious expectations we may have harbored for our children's adulthood, as well as feelings of fear for their future safety. We parents have expectations and fears for all of our children, but our LGBTQ+ children force us to acknowledge them and examine them and transcend them. Which turns out to be a service to our straight children as well.

When your child comes out, you suddenly think less about the inanimate "issues" of LGBTQ+ rights, and more about the flesh-and-blood reality of your child's life. You grasp how your child has truly struggled in coming of age, in the coming-out process, in the risk of telling their truth. You may regret your own cluelessness. I know I do: I regret being blind to the secret pain that had been happening under my roof and under my wing.

A Catholic parent must also come to terms with their Church and the practice of their faith. My life changed when my child came out. I quit my job at a Catholic parish, helped start a local PFLAG group, marched in gay pride parades, encouraged other parents when their children came out, wrote columns in support of marriage equality, and joyfully attended my child's wedding. This did not all happen at once. It's been a process.

I've encountered many companions on the journey: discernment and dialogue, nuance and complexity. And joy. And transformation. And grace. I've also puzzled over our society's, as well as my Church's, mixed messages on inclusion, on homophobia, on diversity and humanity and spirituality. I have fought against the ignorant or mean-spirited proclamations by some Catholic clergy members who should know better— for example, those making the pervasive and theologically unsound assertion that our LGBTQ+ children are, in the very fact of their existence, unworthy of the sacraments. It is no wonder that our children leave a Church that they see as unwelcoming and condemning. They feel that the Church has left them, something that Jesus would not do.

I confess that back when my child first came out, one of my first questions, God forgive me, was whether this might be some sort of phase. A phase! After all the self-searching they had been though, after they bravely came out, what a loathsome thing to be asked by their own mother. Did I think they were suddenly a trend-follower? Had I gone through "a phase" while growing up?

No. I have always known I am straight, just as I have always known I am left-handed. These are not choices I made but how I turned up here on this green earth: God made me straight and gave me recessive genes. I understand that God created my child transgender, just as God created them artistic and tall and witty. I don't accept that God messed up on their creation, that they are wrongly made, or broken. On the contrary, they are "wonderfully made" (Ps 139:14), a beloved child of God.

The path of a parent coming out is not always smooth. A problem I've run up against is that not every adult I know sees my child in the same light that I do. Some, especially those of a fundamentalist bent, view being LGBTQ+ as sinful, as an aberrant choice on a par with perversions like bestiality and pedophilia, or some kind of self-indulgent lark. This shocks me when I compare these summary judgments with the committed, loving, LGBTQ+ people I know. It alarms me to know that there are those who don't even know anyone who is LGBTQ+, but who wish them ill or eternal damnation because of who they are.

Every LGBTQ+ child is unique and different. There is no one way to be LGBTQ+, just as there is no one way to be straight. Correspondingly, every parent's experience is unique and different. But it's up to us parents to show that our love for these children of ours is unwavering, unequivocal, and unconditional. Our children are sensitive, intelligent, talented, delightful, blessed, and LGBTQ+. We stand with them even if we lose some status with our fellow churchgoers in the process. The way we love and support our LGBTQ+ children may even inspire other parents to come out.

When I look at this child of mine, blooming with self-confidence, with comfort, with verve, with true and deep joie de vivre, I am so grateful to be sharing their life. I know in my soul that loving and honoring my wonderfully-made child is exactly in keeping with the message and the work of Jesus Christ.

Climate Crisis

The Eighth Work of Mercy

(2016)

Pope Francis, continuing the work begun in his encyclical on the environment, *Laudato Si'*, has made a radical proposition. On September 1, 2016, which was the second annual Catholic World Day of Prayer for the Care of Creation, he proposed that caring for the earth be designated as an eighth work of mercy.

An eighth work? We Catholics have long memorized the lists of the seven spiritual works of mercy and the seven corporal works of mercy. There are *seven* of each. The spiritual works include such acts as praying for the dead, comforting the sorrowful, and instructing the ignorant in the faith. The corporal works are the ones Jesus lists in Matthew 25: feeding the hungry, clothing the naked, visiting the imprisoned, and such. (We are often better at memorizing than doing, but we aspire to incorporate these good deeds into our daily lives.) Our minds are blown by the idea of an eighth work, because seven is that perfect holy number. What is Pope Francis doing?

Perhaps he is counting on us to stretch ourselves to meet new challenges, and to make the eight-days-a-week effort to clean up the planet-wide messes that we ourselves have caused. Perhaps he hopes that this additional work of mercy, which he calls a "complement to the two traditional sets of seven," can bring about a change of mindset, wherein we are better able to distinguish needs from wants. Perhaps he is encouraging us to reassess our individual responsibility within the greater global good.

In his message on September 1, the pope characterized "care for our common home" as both a spiritual work of mercy—"a grateful contemplation of God's world"—and a corporal work of mercy, entailing "simple daily gestures which break with the logic of violence, exploitation and selfishness." In this vein, the words of St. Teresa of Calcutta come to mind: "In this life we cannot do great things. We can only do small things with great love." The pope refocuses on those small, seemingly insignificant, but practical things previously discussed in *Laudato Si'*, such as turning off the lights, carpooling, recycling waste, planting trees, eating less meat, farming with fewer chemicals, and consuming less of everything.

The spiritual genius of Pope Francis is that he sees the interconnectedness of all life. The grand concepts of social justice, economic justice, and environmental justice are directly related to how we treat each other and how we treat our shared planet. The poor disproportionately suffer the consequences of the sins against creation, the sins of selfishness and exploitation, which are perpetuated by economic and political systems that value profit over people. Love and mercy, on the other hand, apply to everyone and everything. We are to act with mercy, as Jesus did, boundlessly, without mitigation, without hesitation. "The object of mercy," writes Pope Francis, "is human life and everything it embraces." We are to be channels of God's love, which "constantly impels us to find new ways forward."

I have heard certain Catholics call our pope a socialist, as a way of blunting his pointed messages of justice and mercy. With this eighth work of mercy, will they now call him a hippie? *The Washington Post* has referred to the pope's "green agenda," which surely makes these same folks see red. Pope Francis is indeed a bona fide environmentalist, but his concern for the earth exists in the context of respect for the Creator. If we love God, we must also love God's creation: the seas, the clouds, the mountains, the trees, the animals, the people, all of it, every splendid bit. The adjectives "Catholic" and "green," after all, should not be mutually exclusive. As people of faith, part of our work is to conserve and cherish the earthly abode that God had given us. Pope Francis reminds us that this is our calling, eight days a week, to show that we care enough to take those small steps that just might change the world.

Vegetarians for God

(2011)

God blessed them and God said to them, Be fertile and multiply; fill the earth and subdue it. Have dominion over the fish of the sea, the birds of the air, and all the living things that crawl on the earth.

—Genesis 1:28

It's not easy being green.

—Kermit the Frog

I belong to a small minority: vegetarian Catholics.

And I wonder why there are not more of us, because the two commitments strike me as perfectly matched. As a vegetarian,

I believe our human "dominion" does not include killing animals for food. I believe that we are called to respect the integrity of creation by nourishing ourselves more simply, with less wear and tear on the earth, and that vegetarianism is one way to stretch our resources further, to serve the common good more efficiently. As a Catholic, I feel I am honoring the belief that all life is sacred. Not killing any living creature in order to nourish myself seems a natural, logical extension of the "seamless garment" of the Catholic respect for life.

Nevertheless, I have been found wanting both by other Catholics and other vegetarians. Some fellow Catholics, upon hearing I am a vegetarian, assume that I also advocate other suspect liberal positions. They see red (or pinko) flags flying over my head. On the other hand, some fellow vegetarians, upon learning that I am a practicing Catholic, are disappointed that a woman they thought was enlightened is under the influence of the opiate of the masses (or Masses) and therefore must not be a kindred spirit. I am accustomed to being viewed as an outsider by true believers in the two camps to which I passionately believe I belong.

Becoming a vegetarian, like becoming a Catholic, can cause tension in your life. Suddenly, you are different. You get used to not always fitting in, to explaining your beliefs when challenged, to being noticed for your eccentricity. You have faith that you are standing up for a good cause, but you sometimes think wistfully of the days when you were just like everybody else.

It was possibly a random turkey that facilitated our family's transition into vegetarianism. One autumn, over twenty years ago, we made our annual pilgrimage to the pumpkin patch at a local farm. We roamed among the squashes, looking for the perfect jack-o-lantern shape. Beyond the pumpkin patch, in another fenced area, lived a grand and stately turkey. Our three youngsters were drawn to him, his splayed feet and sharp beak and fleshy red wattle. They abandoned us to the pumpkin decision as they peered through the fence and spoke to the turkey. "Gobblegobblegobble," they called, and "Hullo, Mr. Turkey!" For some foolish reason, I said, "Mmmm, there's somebody's nice juicy Thanksgiving dinner."

Why did I say that? We'd been having enough trouble getting our kids to eat meat anyway. They just didn't like it, and I worried about their inadequate protein intake. Horror flashed in my children's eyes as they equated what I made them eat on Thanksgiving with the magnificent creature before them. "We have to rescue him!" cried our preschooler. We explained that he (or probably *she*) belonged to his executioner, as though that made everything all right. Our holiday meal that year felt more like a wake. The little protesters refused to eat the main course and mourned its passing. Soon afterwards, we followed our hearts, bought some cookbooks, and became vegetarians. Twenty-two meatless years and one more baby later, we have yet to succumb to the maladies predicted by my mother, among others.

One burden of going vegetarian, especially for my husband, who loves entertaining, was that our relatives no longer wanted us to host family gatherings. After all, what is Thanksgiving without turkey, Easter without ham, Super Bowl Sunday without cold cut platters? We thought we could cook creatively and treat them to lovely meatless holidays, but the guests had misgivings. We became the people who brought weird stuff to family events, who did not partake of the communal feast. We had ostracized ourselves, nutritionally speaking. By now, people are used to our vegetarian contributions at family celebrations. Sometimes they even try a bite. We also host an annual veggie potluck at our house on World Vegetarian Day in October. Although not in the same league as Thanksgiving, it has become a tradition.

Being Catholic and vegetarian can be a delicate balance. Once, as First Communion time drew near, one of my darlings was concerned that we were called to eat human flesh: surely an animal product! She needed reassurance that one could receive Communion and still be a vegetarian. I tried to explain that none of our fellow Catholics was in fact a cannibal, but transubstantiation is a tricky concept for a child who thinks concretely.

The current perception of global climate change as an environmental as well as a spiritual challenge prompts me to put vegetarianism on the proverbial plate. What is good for the planet is also good for the body human. A few years ago, several of my family members embarked on a three-week cleansing diet that involved eating vegan fare for one week. Much as they didn't like to admit it, they felt better during that week: less sluggish, more focused, healthier. American diets tend to be protein-heavy, and processing such a load taxes our physiological systems. Meat-eaters could survive on a vegan diet one day a month, or, better, one day a week. In these tough economic times, an international advocacy group promotes "Meatless Mondays" as a way to stretch the family food budget while being gentler to the planet. So taking this modest action to save the environment can save one's health, one's waistline, and one's finances. As emotionally difficult as giving up meat can be, neither the human body nor the earth suffers from its absence; in fact, both are more likely to thrive without it.

And I know that what we eat is an emotional issue. We equate our food choices with so many things besides our caloric intake. Food is tangled up in comfort, identity, culture, habit, religion, family, society, celebration, and addiction. Food is intensely personal, in its selection and in its consumption, and nourishes more than the physical human organism. Meat, in particular, is a sign of wealth, of well-being, of satiety, even of patriotism: What meal better precedes American apple pie than meat on the grill?

But a meatless diet makes perfect sense, especially in a world that can easily feed itself without resorting to the slaughter of animals, and without further environmental detriment. As our global future becomes more insecure and ever more fraught with problems, we can't have it both ways: we can't say we care about our environment and yet continue to behave in ways that harm it. The inconsistency reminds me of the people I recently overheard at a restaurant, condemning dog fighting while they were gnawing on someone's ribs and tearing flesh from someone's leg. They were upset about the mistreated dogs, but what about the unfortunate pig on that night's menu? What about the poor chicken? We love our dogs, but we raise and kill millions of animals for food that is actually not good for us. As Mr. Spock of the starship Enterprise would say, that is illogical. And of course, the enlightened Vulcans, the most logical race ever imagined, are vegetarians.

In 2001, the United States Conference of Catholic Bishops issued a statement called *Global Climate Change: A Plea for Dialogue, Prudence, and the Common Good*. A 12-page document that examines Catholic social teaching in relation to climate change, it has this to say about the stewardship of the planet bestowed by God:

"True stewardship requires changes in human actions—both in moral behavior and technical advancement. Our religious tradition has always urged restraint and moderation in the use of material goods, so we must not allow our desire to possess more material things to overtake our concern for the basic needs of people and the environment. . . . Changes in lifestyle based on traditional moral virtues can ease the way to a sustainable and equitable world economy in which sacrifice will no longer be an unpopular concept. For many of us, a life less focused on material gain may remind us that we are more than what we have. . . . A renewed sense of sacrifice and restraint could make an essential contribution to addressing global climate change."

All these years later, sacrifice is still an unpopular concept, but the years have added urgency to these excellent suggestions. I must note, however, that reducing or eliminating the consumption of meat still does not always make the list of recommended, sustainable ways to go green.

A potential pitfall of a vegetarian lifestyle is the temptation to treat the body as God rather than temple: "Do you not know," asks St. Paul in his first letter to the Corinthians, "that you are the temple of God, and that the Spirit of God dwells in you? . . . [T]he temple of God, which you are, is holy" (3:16-17). In our society, we routinely desecrate the temple: We chop up and rearrange our bodies to make them more attractive. We inflate our breasts and tuck our tummies and stretch our wrinkles. We overeat, we starve ourselves, we pump up on steroids. We abuse our bodies with little thought for the God who dwells within. Perversely, though, we can arrive at a point where we worship the body, putting physical, ephemeral needs above everything else, and forget about God. When we are vegetarian zealots, food philosophers, what we eat can become a religion unto itself. Without the balance of body and spirit, our world becomes too narrow. Worst of all, we are tempted to retreat from the greater community, the other temple referred to by Paul (Eph 2:21-22), by focusing only on ourselves.

In the era of climate change, the personal is political. The dietary choices we make, along with all other consumption of resources, have serious and evident consequences. When our concerns are small and self-centered, when we do not bind the local to the global, or the physical to the spiritual, we work against the common good. If we are to be God's true temple, we need to be built up, cleaned up, and smartened up.

The growing Catholic awareness of the issues of climate change, environmental fragility, and spiritual responsibility gives me hope that times are changing. A parish I recently visited advertised a "Green Bible" for sale in the parish gift shop. "The Green Bible encourages people to see God's vision for creation and helps us in healing and sustaining it," enthused the blurb in the bulletin. The Society of Jesus published a special report on ecology called "Healing a Broken World," which calls on Jesuits worldwide to "cast a grateful look on creation, letting our hearts be touched by its wounded reality and making a strong personal and communal commitment to healing it." The report asks Jesuits to evaluate their own life choices in light of social justice and environmental concerns, and to promote local and global solutions that are practical, spiritual, ethical, and green. Increasingly, we grasp that the thoughtful stewardship of all creation is a calling from God. Conscious care for the earth is intrinsic to caring for each other.

We humans are hungry for truth, for sacred connection, for what is holy, for what lasts. The way we feed our bodies can also feed our souls. I suppose we Catholics will know that true conversion of heart has taken place when the Knights of Columbus hold a veggie fry for charity.

Injustice in the System/Violence

To Life!

(2000)

Will you sign the petition for a moratorium on the death penalty?" I ask an elderly gentleman, a fellow parishioner. My friend Dolores and I are gathering signatures after all the Masses this weekend to ask the United Nations to pass a resolution calling for a worldwide moratorium on the death penalty.

He wrinkles his nose at me, as though I smell bad. "I can't agree with that," he says.

"Can I give you a pamphlet to read, explaining what the Holy Father has said?" I ask hopefully. It is early in the day.

"No," he says. "Not interested."

Another man, a father of four and seemingly mild-mannered, is taking Dolores to task for even asking for his signature on such a misguided petition. "You have one quote!" he says. "What about all the encyclicals of the past? What about the teaching of history? Don't bother me with this!" He storms away, his day possibly ruined by being accosted by fools outside his beloved church.

"You mean the encyclical about the Inquisition?" I whisper to her. She smiles. But we are both a bit shaken.

We expected a buzz, knew that we'd be stirring up the hornet's nest. Aside from the statistics that show that most American Catholics support the death penalty and would in fact be willing to pull the switch themselves, we live in a town whose main industry is a state prison. The prison is our bread and butter, but it takes a toll on our compassion. "If you saw what I see . . ." one guard tells us wearily. And we are tongue-tied in our response to the jaded daily reality of this person.

Yet five or six other guards sign our petition. Still others stay clear of our table, turning a deaf ear to our invitation.

Next to us, on the same weekend, is a table where registered voters can sign to make it illegal (it is currently legal) in California for a minor to have an abortion without a parent's knowledge or consent. Their table is mobbed. People discuss the issue with emphatically nodding heads and jabbing fingers and hands folded in prayer. Everyone agrees on this one. At their table, they run out of forms. They can't pass around pens fast enough. At our table, where you don't have to be a registered voter to sign, where you don't even have to be eighteen or a U.S. citizen, we have many blank lines. We lend them our pens.

I explain our petition to a teenage girl who waits idly while her mother signs the minor abortion initiative. The girl is about to sign in support of the moratorium but hesitates when her mother joins her. "Don't be ridiculous," her mother snaps. "We NEED capital punishment." The girl is led away to the family van.

The refusal of so many to sign the moratorium petition gives an ironic twist to the phrase "cafeteria Catholic." Some of the pillars of the parish, those considered devout Catholics, sometimes hurl the epithet of "cafeteria Catholic" at those who use birth control or who miss Mass on holy days of obligation.

But they are themselves refusing one of the Catholic side dishes when it comes to the death penalty. As one fellow says, brushing past me, "We don't need no more of that *Dead Man Walking* crap."

The "consistent ethic of life," of which Cardinal Bernardin wrote so movingly, holds that all life is sacred, from conception to natural death. A guilty life is still sacred life in the eyes of God. In this pro-life spirit, one would assume Catholics would move from one table to the other without pause. To sign one's name for life means to sign against abortion as well as against the death penalty. To do otherwise is to deny the redemptive power of God's love for us all. But it is much easier to side with innocent life than with life that has itself taken life. "An eye for an eye" is a phrase we hear frequently. No arguing with the Bible. But as Dolores points out gently, "God did not kill Cain."

And what about Jesus, himself a victim of the death penalty, who preached and practiced forgiveness, who came for sinners? Dolores repeats the words of Mother Teresa, which she has posted on a sign on the wall behind us, "Do what Jesus would do."

"I have a tough time with this one," says one woman, as she signs for the moratorium.

"So do I," sighs her friend, who does not sign.

"My son was a soldier! He killed in the war!" says a mother. "Is he wrong?" *Oh Lord*, we think. *That's another petition, isn't it?*

"I will sign against the death penalty," says another mother, who has had trouble with her boy. "Otherwise, how do I know I am not signing my own son's death warrant?" Another unimagined angle, at least on my part.

At the end of the day, we have 121 signatures to send to the moratorium organization, who will then send them on to the United Nations. We feel a little bruised, Dolores and I, but also happy for the signatures gathered. When we remember what martyrs have endured for the sake of their faith, we feel silly. We have hardly been persecuted. We've rather been both annoyed and annoying: gnats among saints.

Granted, 121 is but a fraction of the nearly 1,000 families registered in our parish. But the 121 signatures have been freely given by some of the most love-filled people I know. More important, perhaps, are the pamphlets we have pressed into sometimes unwilling hands. The death penalty cuts off the possibility of a perpetrator's conversion. But maybe later tonight, in the cocoon of a reading chair, maybe just one heart will experience a fluttering conversion of its own. For such epiphanies we can only pray to the Lord of life.

Ashes in Parkland

(2018)

The sun rises as I retrieve Thursday's *Los Angeles Times* from my driveway. On the front page, the indelible image from yesterday's high school shooting in Parkland, Florida, is of a woman, presumably a mother, crying, her arm clasped tight around a teenage student. The forehead of this present-day Madonna wears the vestige of a black cross, drawn in ashes. The photo makes me relive, as strongly as a slap, the cross that was traced on my own forehead only yesterday. The accompanying news story describes how seventeen people were shot dead and at least a dozen others were wounded. It was Valentine's Day. For us Catholics, it was also Ash Wednesday.

The ashes that mark our foreheads only last for a day, but the ashes on our hearts are meant to endure for the entire 40 days of Lent and beyond. We receive our ashes as a sign of repentance, of our yearning for God's forgiveness, of our intent to live our faith more truly in the face of our mortality. "Remember you are dust, and to dust you will return," says the priest or lay minister, blessing us with a blackened thumb.

How sadly, tragically, wretchedly fitting is the front-page photo from this Ash Wednesday.

Again, again. Once again in our gun-adoring nation, students and teachers, supposedly safe at school, are never coming home. Once again, parents and family members wait with dread to learn if their dear sweet loved ones are among the dead. Once again, we hear people say how they never thought this would happen in their community. At their school. To their neighbors, their coaches, their teachers, their children. Once again, our nation needs to repent of our ways, and turn away from sin.

May we repent, and may God forgive us, as we worship at the altar of the gun, even to the point of sacrificing our own children. May we repent, and may God forgive us, as we allow the moneyed lobbyists to speak for us and to subvert the popular will to curtail the ubiquity of military-style weapons among us. May we repent, and may God forgive us, as we offer "thoughts and prayers" that cost us nothing instead of real and lasting answers to the hatred we bear each other, to the fears that drive us to kill, to the violence that permeates our lives.

And may we find the strength to overcome our feelings of helplessness and hopelessness: because just like after every mass shooting, most of us Americans will sympathize with the pain of the bereaved families and then move on with our own lives. We shield ourselves from the thought of the missing faces at the dinner table, at Easter, at graduation, of the teenagers who will never be a day older, of the educators who did the brave things their calling compelled them to do for their students, of the dozens of funerals soon to take place in each new stricken town. It's all too much. There are so many tragic news stories about the guns that, in spite of the NRA's rhetoric, do kill people, children, students, teachers, spouses, soldiers, young people, old people, sad people, innocent people. We have compassion-fatigue, or maybe compassion-overload. We turn off our empathy. We can hardly bear to think of the most-recent dead as our own. So we don't.

But today, with ashes faded from our foreheads but not from our hearts, let us think of them. Let us claim them as our own. Let us hold them gently in our mind's eye. Let us pause and mourn their lives abruptly ended. Let us promise them that we will honor their memories by engaging in fruitful solutions to the social ills that plague our country and steal too many lives. And lest we get bogged down in shouting matches over legalities, let us resurrect our capacity for both empathy and action. Let us stand on the common ground of love.

Lent is for starting over, but some things can't be redone. We cannot wake the dead, but perhaps we can step onto the road of repentance by actively seeking God's mercy. If we pray to be instruments of God's peace, maybe we can start by not letting our surviving children down. The cross of ashes on the front page cries out for us to trudge the road to Lenten forgiveness with faith, with purpose, with persistence of heart, with trust in the God who loves us hugely in spite of our sins.

System of Injustice

(2017)

O n a Friday morning in June, I am driving too fast on a freeway south. My daughter has been in jail since last night. The bail bondsman I call from my car answers on the first ring.

I give him an arrest number. He puts me on hold. A recording of Frank Sinatra sings about flying away with him, a seemingly inappropriate sentiment for this business.

He comes back on the line. He is reassuring, soothing. He can free my daughter today. He just needs some paperwork: my most recent pay stub, my tax return—

I cut him off, panicky. I am already twenty miles from home, and I don't travel with these documents.

"Why do you need those?" I ask. "Can't I just give you money?"

"You gonna pay $2,000 up front?" he asks, surprised.

"Don't I have to?" I am naive in the intricacies of posting bail. I work in a prison, but I haven't been on this side of things before.

He recovers his cool, realizing he is talking to one of those rare and lucky Americans with a savings account.

"I won't need those if you can pay the ten percent," he says. "Two thousand. Plus the filing fees."

And that's what I do. But since then, I've learned that if I didn't have that kind of cash on hand, I would have to put up collateral, such as my house or my car, and make payments at a hefty interest rate. If I weren't able to do any of that, my loved one would simply sit in jail, pre-trial, pre-anything, supposedly innocent until proven guilty, but doing time nevertheless.

Welcome to the money bail system.

The bondsman explains to me that I will never see that payment again, no matter what happens with my daughter's case, even if it is dismissed: that is the agency's fee for doing the dirty work of bailing her out. Which, he reminds me, they are experts at. If she doesn't check in with the bondsman weekly, or if she misses a court date, I will owe the entire $20,000. If I want to save the bond agency's fee and post twenty grand directly with the court, I can navigate the system myself, but he assures me that the court will find a way to keep my deposit forever. One little technical slip-up, and my money evaporates. Do I want to risk that?

Well, no. When I finally get to his office, I transfer the funds, hand over my debit card, sign papers, affix my thumbprint to one of them, and promise to bring my daughter to this office as soon as she is released. This is all done by about 3:00 p.m.

I meet my daughter's boyfriend, alias Nate, at the jailhouse.

"It looks like you are at the County Jail. Would you like to check in?" Facebook asks me.

Um, no, Facebook. I would not like to broadcast that I am at the County Jail to bail out my daughter. Two well-dressed, solicitous men outside the parking structure ask if we need help getting somebody released. Bail bondsmen. Sort of like ambulance chasers, only they approach people who look disoriented and freaked out. But I have already handed $2,020 to a guy named Ray. The $2,000 is ten percent of the $20,000 set for her bail amount, and the $20 is the court fee for processing the $2,000. I think.

Nate and I approach the reception window, but it's hard to see the person inside. He yells at us for not standing in the right line, and then for not approaching quickly enough, for wasting his precious time. We are still under the fantasy that my daughter will be released at any moment. The officer tells us to take a seat.

The paperwork proceeds at the county-mandated glacial pace.

We sit in the waiting room. This is too generous a term for this area, because it is one of the most un-ergonomically designed places I have ever waited, starting with this uncomfortable plastic chair. I assume the hard plastic, which is mounted on a concrete base, is ideal for its slash-proof, stain-proof, vomit-proof, and maybe even graffiti-proof qualities, although I can't imagine anyone trying to get away with anything when they can't see where the officer behind the black glass is looking. I imagine this entire waiting room can be hosed down.

The officer in the booth calls us back, yells at us to go downstairs to prove the bail has been posted, then yells at us not to take our personal stuff with us, but to avail ourselves of the coin-operated lockers to stash our belongings. I am grateful that I still carry around loose change, because of course he can't help us with the necessary quarters. I don't know why the yelling is necessary, other than to establish that we are not friends. Or that those of us on the other side of his impenetrable glass are not human beings.

We go downstairs to the cashier to make sure all is in order. I produce my paperwork with my daughter's arrest number, with the record of my payment. After some shuffling of forms, we learn that all is in order for her release. We just have to wait. Shouldn't be too long. It's maybe five or six o'clock by this time, still light outside, a Friday turning into the weekend for normal people.

We wait. We talk. We learn a lot about each other. We discuss alcoholism and addiction and my daughter's mental breakdown that has led to her arrest. Nate periodically goes outside, gets some air, uses his phone, walks around, gives some quarters to a hapless lady being yelled at by the reception officer so she can stow her purse. The hours of sitting around doing nothing are impossible for him. I chat a little with a young woman who has just bailed out her brother again. "He's a good kid," she says. "Just confused, maybe. And now he's going to lose his job."

Women arrive in waves to surrender themselves to the authorities, showing up to serve prearranged jail sentences. We watch as a parade of down-on-their-luck women, some crying, some a little drunk, are processed into jail by female officers.

The female officers also yell at, smirk at, and insult their charges before leading them into the bowels of the jail. These officers are tightly wound, from their hair slicked back into buns to their thin-set mouths to their perfectly creased uniforms. They are tall and intimidating, and they seem to like their roles as much as they dislike the women they incarcerate.

Evening becomes night. People are released, but not my daughter. The newly freed immediately check their phones, and curse when the phones are dead. An old woman borrows Nate's phone to call for her ride, which is not here as promised. The driver on the other end is confused by the unknown number turning out to be her mother. The daughter is also lost in the maze of streets outside the jail complex. The old woman asks Nate to explain to her daughter how to get here, but it doesn't go well. Nate goes outside to try to direct her or flag her down or something. The woman seems way too old to have broken the law.

The brother of the young woman is released. He is terribly young and quite annoyed and dressed in drag. Maybe that's what she meant by "confused." His eyes are smudged with fatigue and the remains of a smoky eye.

A woman tries to turn herself in, but she has missed the deadline. The reception officer yells at her that it's like ten o'clock and she's in a heap of trouble. She begins to cry, says she's late because the care she'd arranged for her child was late. Touchingly, he stops yelling. But he still won't admit her.

A few more people are released in a trickle. Not my daughter. Then, at around 11:30, something strange happens. A whole bunch of people come into the waiting room to claim their troublemakers. It's as if they know exactly when to show up to pick up their loved ones. They've done this before. Nate and I are the only saps who believed the timeline we'd been told. A whole bunch of people are suddenly released.

My daughter is released around midnight.

She emerges from lockup moving like a frail old lady, although she is in her twenties. She has two black eyes. She is wearing a paper shirt. Her pants are as waterlogged as when they'd been shoved into a plastic bag more than a day ago. When she sees us, she starts crying. My heart breaks into pieces.

"Why are you here?" she asks me.

"Because I'm your mom," I say, holding her shivering body against me. "Somebody had to bail you out," I say, trying not to cry myself.

"But you said you would never . . ."

That's when I remember telling my teenage children that if they ever got arrested, they could expect to stay in jail, because I wasn't going to bail them out. Unless they were protesting for a good cause: then I would rescue them. If they'd simply misbehaved and gotten caught, they could suffer the consequences.

I'd forgotten my own rules. That mom didn't know a whole lot, I think. That mom didn't understand how complicated life could get.

"I need help," she says piteously. Nate and I nod at the obvious.

"I'm going to a meeting," she says. (Months later, Nate tells me that their entire relationship was riding on what she said when she was released. If she'd come out with her usual bravado, trash-talking the cops and full of self-righteousness, he was gone. Instead, he went to Al-Anon.)

We drive over to check in with the bail guy. At one in the morning, it's a different bail guy, but the place is brightly lit, open for business. My daughter has to sign more papers, and surrender her fingerprints, and make many promises. Nate takes her home. They invite me to stay with them overnight, but I tell them I am going to drive home.

I change my mind as I start the drive. I am beyond tired. Around 2:00 a.m., for the first time in my life, I check into a hotel with nothing. No reservation. No luggage. Who does that? I think I look suspicious, but the clerk is unfazed. I ask for a complimentary toothbrush. It has been a day of firsts. I sleep in my underwear so I can hang my clothes up and wear them home in the morning with some shred of respectability. I dream a lot of dreams that do not stay long enough for me to remember them, but that disturb me anyway. I check out after less than one full night's stay.

As I drive home, I feel a little guilty, a little dirty. The method by which my daughter got out of jail feels shameful. If I didn't have that money available, or a way to beg for or borrow the cash, my daughter would remain in jail at least through the weekend. On Monday, a judge might have released her on her own recognizance. And if that didn't happen, and it probably wouldn't have, she would have sat in that hellhole until at least her first court date, which was a month later. There are people in this country of ours who are behind bars for months and years, who have not been convicted of any charges, who are awaiting their day in court, and whose only crime to that point is basically lacking wealth. While they are locked up, their financial problems deepen. They may lose their job or housing or car or even custody of their children.

Proposed legislation in many jurisdictions to abolish the money bail system is mightily opposed by the bail bond industry. Some reforms would ensure that judges can determine, in the interest of public safety rather than a bank balance, who can be released while they await trial. Some would also provide pretrial services to help people get back to court and comply with the judge's conditions of release.

Freedom should not belong only to those who can purchase it. As grateful as I was to be able to bail my daughter out of jail, the level of privilege that made her freedom possible sickens me. This is not right. This is not justice.

How do we count our privileges? Making bail is one. At my daughter's first appearance in front of a judge, he offers her a deal: three years' probation, a fine, ten weeks of anger management, two of four misdemeanors dropped, surrender a DNA sample. The catch is that she must decide to take it or leave it immediately and forfeit her right to an attorney. She would also lose the right to explain anything to the court or to speak on her own behalf. He also notes, in a pleasant but vaguely ominous tone, that if she doesn't take the offer, the next one may be worse. He makes this offer to everyone, all thirty or so other offenders in the courtroom, who are also awaiting their moment of reckoning.

Our next privilege is that we have with us a friend of the family who is a public defender in another county. He can't represent her, but we can pick his brains. We are ready to take the deal, since it does not involve jail time, which is my daughter's biggest fear. But he explains that the deal is not great. Probation means submitting to warrantless searches at any time for three years. It means a conviction record. He also says that in his county, it is standard procedure to speak to a public defender before seeing the judge, and this system smells bad to him. "You should never forfeit your right to counsel," he says.

We are pretty nervous to turn the deal down, but my daughter does it.

She is the only one in the courthouse that day not to take the deal.

Without our friend's expertise, we would have definitely taken the deal, because what do we know? We are not lawyers. Which is why we need one.

The harried public defender who finally meets with my daughter over the next several weeks negotiates a much better deal for her: no jail, no probation, payment for damages, anger management classes, DNA sample. If she completes these steps satisfactorily, her record will be expunged. Months later, when all of this has been accomplished and documented, along with regular AA meetings, my repentant and clear-eyed daughter stands in front of a different judge. This judge raises an eyebrow at the lenient terms to which the prosecutor has agreed. More privilege, the eyebrow says.

And I agree. There are two systems of justice at work in our country, one for people with resources, and one for those without. As beneficiaries of the first, it is on us to speak out against and find ways to rectify the second.

The Privilege of Skin
(2021)

How to start this essay? Maybe with a proposal: If you are a white person who doesn't believe white privilege is a thing, keep reading. Humor me. I can explain white privilege to you, because I have lived it. I have taken it for granted all my life.

I was born to white parents in a white neighborhood. Thus begins white privilege. I did not earn the right to be a baby in a middle-class American family, but there I was. I was loved and fed and housed and educated in a safe environment. If my parents struggled to pay the bills, I didn't know it. My dad went to college on the G.I. Bill. My folks got approved for a home mortgage. At school, I was a regular kid. Nothing about my appearance made me seem dangerous or different to others. If you grew up similarly, you benefited from white privilege.

I got older, got good grades, went on family vacations, made and lost friends, survived adolescence, learned to drive, learned about sex, had my heart broken, got into college, all the usual things. I heard about prejudice in our society, but I didn't live it. I never suspected the world was not my oyster. Because it was. Sure, life bumped and bruised me, but I assumed my future would work out fine. I belonged, without question, everywhere I went. That was my unexamined white privilege, and maybe yours, too. We didn't do anything wrong. We were just white in the United States.

But those of us born into such privilege must now look at our lives with eyes wide open. Rather than writing words of blame, I hope instead to shine some light on how white privilege has obscured our vision and made us unaware of injustices that, even if we have not personally perpetuated them, have been happening in front of our faces.

Wonder with me: What would it have been like if, when I was a kid, Santa Claus and his helpers were Black? If all Barbies and Kens were Black? If all Disney princesses were Black? If everyone in government and all the faces on TV were Black? If God was Black? If Jesus was Black? My white childhood would have been completely different. My obvious whiteness would have set me apart, skewed my self-image. I would have known I didn't fit in, that I wasn't meant to be part of this society, that people like me were unwelcome and even feared. All by the time I finished grade school.

My family might have taught me to expect name-calling and bigotry and random undeserved hatred, and to swallow my reaction to mistreatment because if I protested, the situation would get way worse. I was to keep a civil tongue in my head and my gaze neutral and my hands visible on the steering wheel if I were pulled over by the police. Because being white, I would definitely get pulled over by the police many times. I was to understand that some unenlightened people would credit my accomplishments to affirmative action or preferential treatment or minority quotas. And I was to let it all go for the sake of maintaining the precarious peace of my existence.

That's what it must be like, for starters, to live without white privilege. Not that we can know. We are not subject to systemic racism.

Here's more evidence of my white privilege: when my white daughter, in a manic blackout incident, was arrested by cops with their guns drawn, she was not shot dead. I'm pretty sure this wasn't luck; the color of her skin saved her life. I hadn't taught any of my kids how to act around the police so they would not be killed. White privilege means that it never occurred to me to do so. If you've never had that talk with your kids, you own white privilege, too.

Here's a white-privilege Facebook post: "Have you ever noticed that the police leave you alone if you aren't doing anything illegal?" This only applies to white folks. Black people get shot in their own homes, even in their own beds. See the deaths of Botham Jean or Breonna Taylor, among many others, who were deemed a threat because they were Black.

Here's a haunting BLM protest sign: "How Many Are Not Filmed?" White privilege means that we don't fear police misconduct or have to rely on cell-phone footage for any prayer of justice prevailing. We believe the police are here to help us. And when we call them, they actually do help us.

Blindness to my white privilege makes me part of the problem. But rather than get defensive, here's what I must remember: My rights are not diminished when someone else's are protected. My life is not threatened when someone else's is respected. My voice is not silenced when someone else's is heard. My history is not erased when someone else's is taught.

Same goes for you, if you're still with me. Clearly, we must work harder to change course. If fear has made us cling to our privilege, we must be braver. If ignorance has insulated us, we must listen and learn. To take the higher road at this American crossroads, we must step into other shoes.

Aging

Evil to Graceful in 60 Seconds

(2005)

At two years from 50 and counting, I am perimenopausal. The prefix "peri" attached to a noun, means *around* or *about*, as in "perimeter" or "pericardium." This does not, however, apply to "periwinkle," which is one of my favorite crayons. I am intrigued by another definition of the word "peri," which, according to Persian mythology, is a superhuman being, originally portrayed as evil, but later represented as a graceful fairy. That about sums up my experience of perimenopause: I can go from evil to graceful in 60 seconds or less. And then back.

The definition of menopause is not, contrary to popular belief, "to take a pause from men," although that might be a sound treatment option for some menopausal symptoms. It is, rather, "the cessation of menstruation." While this sounds like an excellent idea to an active 16-year-old, it is a far more complicated and delicate issue for a woman of my advancing years. It means the end of a chapter. The end of an era. The end of the possibility, however nonsensical or unwished-for, of another child. I am becoming a woman no longer capable of giving birth.

Thus is my state defined: "around or about the cessation of menstruation." I am definitely perimenopausal. Pleased to meet you.

Here is my perimenopausal morning: I wake up with cramps (I thought I was too old for cramps), but stoically decide to go for a run anyway. As I step out the front door, I am greeted by a sea of unfurled toilet paper and plastic forks where there was once a front lawn. Barely a blade of grass is visible. The toilet paper has been draped and crumpled and shredded and is leaking into the street. The forks are a bizarre touch, and they stab me as I scoop up handfuls of dew-damp paper. As I stuff the leavings into a trash bag, I am overcome with emotions: sadness at the wanton waste of trees and paper, nostalgia for the days when my children's friends were too young to TP a house, and irritation at this messy adolescent ritual, which in my increasingly incensed opinion is but one step above the male baboon showing off his big red butt. I realize I am near tears. I am in despair, for the world is a place without hope. Then, instantly, I laugh at my ridiculous overreaction. Why am I so upset? Instead of a police officer at the door with terrible, horrible news, it's just toilet paper. My loved ones are safe, my house is undamaged. I laugh loudly, uncontrollably, maniacally. My world has not collapsed, but my emotional state is close to it.

I don't go for a run. I waddle with my load of waste to the trash can. Then I sit out back with a cup of chamomile tea for my cramps, praying for balance.

I knew about the hot flashes and the sweats, the thin hair and the dry membranes, the brittle bones and the wrinkles. I was prepared for the physical manifestations of menopause, and indeed some have happened. What I was not ready for was the emotional instability, the mental spaciness, the swinging moods. I have not felt this dangerously out of control since I was pregnant.

My two younger daughters are still talking about the day at the burger joint. We were finishing our fries, and my girls were imitating something I'd said, or the way I'd said it, which is one of their favorite games. They truly do not do this maliciously, and usually I don't mind playing the uncool mom, but for some reason, at this particular moment, their words seemed cruel. I suddenly felt unbearably sad and hurt. I stood up and told them I'd wait for them in the car. They watched in amazement as I did just that. When they joined me after a few minutes, they were speechless. It was an awkward drive home. What was up with Mom?

They don't remember the strange emotions and fluctuating hormones of pregnancy, when I sobbed at the sight of a man eating a bowl of soup alone in a restaurant, or when I watched sentimental commercials, or whenever groups of children sang. My husband, though, is probably having déjà vu. At least this time, he doesn't have to go to natural childbirth classes. At least when this phase is over, there won't be a wee person waking him up by night and draining his bank account by day. There won't be a new baby to steal his heart and ask for another storybook in the big chair and make him dance by the light of the moon . . .

Great. Time for my latest crying jag.

I suspect that my sense of womanliness has been tied up in motherhood for so long that the thought of losing the ability to become a mother is akin to losing my identity as a woman. Even though I know that is absurd. Even though, at this age, I have no desire for another newborn infant. Even though on most days I am comfortable with who I am. Even though. Even though.

I feel like I have one last labor to do. I still have to pass through the birth canal of menopause. My (slightly) older friends tell me that on the other side, a pool of calm and peace awaits. They say there is also spice and adventure and good sex. There is laughter and wisdom and acceptance and true freedom, with never the need to buy another feminine paper product. When this crazed birthing is over, my last, best self will have been born, the final chapter in a life of joy and surprises. I'm hoping it's a long one.

It Takes a Village

(2013)

My mother now lives in a place called "The Village," and if it takes a village to raise a child, it certainly seems to take a village for our family to care for our mother. (I was tempted to write "to lower our mother," as in the opposite of "to raise," but the funereal connotation is too unpleasant.)

My mother lives in the part of The Village subtitled "assisted living," which implies that she needs help breathing or maintaining a pulse. She does not, but she does need a level of intimate care that we, her six children, could no longer safely or ably provide. My father died four years ago, and my mother lived with (and paid the mortgage for) one of my sisters. When my sister was daunted by the daily demands of living with an incontinent, forgetful, 80-year-old woman with Parkinson's disease, the decision was made to sell the house and use the proceeds to move my mother to The Village. I do not mean to imply that this decision was lightly made: it took a couple of years, several falls, many accusatory emails, a series of biting meetings, and a visit from the police. My sister's family is now an estranged branch of the family tree. You could say it didn't go well. But I digress.

When we visit our mother at The Village, we go to the right side of the building; the left side houses the folks who are still capable of "independent living," although they too have no need to do any cooking or working or cleaning or gardening or driving or the many other tasks they accomplished on a daily basis when they were younger. I imagine that if you don't require the kind of assistance my mother does, living at The Village would be sort of like being on a cruise for the rest of your life, because on both sides of The Village, there are exercise classes, craft activities, poker, bingo, trivia games, an internet café, a pool, a movie theater, happy hours, special events like luaus, lectures, concerts, day trips, holiday celebrations, discussion groups, and book circles, sometimes all in the same day. You can gauge an event's popularity by the number of walkers parked just outside the venue. Three meals a day, light on salt and sugar, are served in the dining room by waiters and waitresses, all of whom are candidates for sainthood. Several times a day, good-natured health aides bring around little cups of pills like hors d'oeuvres. On the assisted living side, the aides also dress the residents, shower them, change their soiled clothing and bedding, help them in and out of bed, bandage their scrapes, monitor their vital signs, escort them to the dining room when they get turned around, and arrive promptly at the door when a summoning button is pushed. They are everywhere, and unfailingly sweet. They network via walkie-talkie. Their system works.

So my mother, after six months of residency, is comfortable, cared for, physically safe, mentally engaged, and socially active. Her color and her mobility have improved. In some ways, she is part of an elder gang: she and her fellow inhabitants at The Village have formed a quasi-family of similarly challenged folks who exist on the edge of society. Sometimes when I visit—and my mother has frequent visitors, unlike some of her new friends—I feel guilty that we did not simply absorb her into one of our homes. Three of my siblings live out-of-state, and the one who lives closest to our mother has two toddlers, which leaves the one who tried and failed to care for her and no longer speaks to anyone, and me. I live about a hundred miles north, and my mother often stated that she would not be content in my small, boring, cold-weather town, but still. I feel that I have failed to live up to the multi-generational ideal for a functional family, of providing a home where the wise grandmother enriches the daily life of her offspring's family with wit and grace, of caring for an aging parent with the same love and attention with which she once cared for me. Instead, I have warehoused my mother.

And once again, God's boundless sense of humor infuses my life with the last thing I'd ever expect to happen: my mother, safely moved into an assisted living facility, needing help with the most unmentionable of personal tasks, has a beau. I'll call him Jerome. The staff members are a bit flummoxed by this blossoming relationship, which they say has never come up on the assisted living side before. I infer from them that the independent living side is a regular Peyton Place. My mother and Jerome, who is a recent widower, spend a lot of time together at daily activities. She watches *Jeopardy!* and *Wheel of Fortune* in his room every night. They share snacks. They embrace and hold hands, and they kiss goodbye when I pick my mother up for an outing or an errand or a doctor's appointment. To my dismay, and knowing full well I should be happy for my mother's newfound companionship, I secretly compare Jerome to my dad and find Jerome lacking. I have sad insight into what it must feel like to be a child of divorce.

"What do you think of Jerome?" my mother asks me coyly, like we are eighth graders.

"He's nice," I say.

"He asked me to be his girlfriend," she says.

"Well, I'm not going to call him 'Dad,' " I tell her, and immediately feel bad. Why would I deny her the joy of Jerome? What is my problem? If I say I want my mother to be happy in her golden years, why am I resentful when she is?

And once again: always an opportunity for new growth in my spiritual development, for new acceptance of God's presence in all things, for new depth to my soul.

My mother's photo regularly appears in The Village's monthly newsletter, often at Jerome's side, always smiling and doing something entertaining. She is becoming a fixture there, in a way that she would probably not be in one of her children's spare rooms. It is becoming her home, a home away from any home we ever shared with her, a home where we are visitors. I watch her shrink, in body and in mind, as she travels the road of age and illness, and I wonder if we have done the right thing. She has the funds to afford another ten years at The Village, at least, and so we will worry about where she will live after that when that time comes. Which is when our family will have to become the village that she needs.

A Thankless Child

(2015)

My mother's Parkinson's disease is having its merciless way with her. She uses a walker for stability, but she has fallen several times, always because she thought she'd "just do this one little thing" without her walker, only to lose her balance and land hard on the floor. After each incident, her nagging children have told her: "Don't do anything without your walker! You don't want to break a hip!" Then we watch her toddle off to do "one little thing" right under our noses. Parkinson's is characterized by a shuffling walk, and in my mother's case, it has robbed her of the ability to pivot on the ball of her foot, thus causing her to lose her bearings and tumble when she tries to turn. But no amount of our nagging seemed to impress on her the seriousness of her falling.

So one day in August, alone in her room at her assisted living facility, my mother must have thought she'd just do that one little thing, and fell. And broke her hip. She doesn't remember doing this, dementia also being a symptom of Parkinson's.

She is now very upset with us, her children, for leaving her in a strange place, which is a rehab facility post-surgery. She is not cognizant of the miracle that she personifies: she has survived a fall, a broken hip, hip replacement surgery, general anesthesia, morphine, and a stubborn staph infection, before being moved to this place she loathes. For an 83-year-old, falling and breaking a hip can be a death sentence. But my mother, against all odds, is recovering. She is taking tentative steps with a walker and a physical therapist as a spotter. My mother may yet be able to return to her familiar home, to her friends and her activities and her boyfriend.

My siblings and I realize, however, that she will need full-time care in addition to the assisted living. Assisted living means that she has her meals prepared, her medication managed, her room cleaned, her laundry done, and her personal hygiene attended to by friendly and competent health care aides. But she also has a lot of freedom during the day. She can choose from various activities, take advantage of services like manicures and hairdressing, hang out with friends, or spend time in her room alone. It's that last part that won't fly. We see that without constant supervision, she will fall again.

These are the decisions adult children often must make for an aging parent. My mother is fortunate that my dad left her well-off financially, but her wealth is finite. And what if she did not have money in the bank? The choices narrow without means. Just after my mother's surgery, when she first arrived at the rehab facility and was in pretty bad shape, when her infection was raging and her ability to swallow food was compromised—another feature of the cruel Parkinson's—a hospice representative approached my sister. Actually, she overwhelmed my sister. Hospice workers cared for my dad in the last few days of his life, and they were thorough, understanding, and wonderful for him and for the family. This one was different. She presented hospice in hard-sell fashion, as though the only smart option was taking our mother home and making her comfortable until she expired. The hospice rep was the naysayer to any positive development in our mother's condition, right up until our mother improved enough that she was no longer a candidate for hospice.

The pressure my sister felt from the hospice rep made me wonder: What if my mother didn't have adequate funding for a future of expensive care? What if my sister hadn't had siblings and friends with whom to talk through the situation and the options? What if she'd acquiesced to the hospice person to sign our mother up for end-of-life, palliative care? Quite possibly, we would now be planning our mother's funeral.

And then the terrible thought lurks: Would that have been kinder for my mother?

My mother's Parkinson's disease is never going to get better; it will progress to something worse. Right now she is alone and miserable where she is, even though we all visit her. When it's time to leave, she cries and begs each of us to take her home. Heartbroken, we explain that the situation is temporary, that she can leave this place as soon as she is strong enough, but she doesn't get it. She forgets the facts. She gets belligerent. She feels abandoned, abused, unloved, no matter what we say or do. Every visit ends badly. On one occasion, as I am saying goodbye, she quotes Shakespeare at me: *How sharper than a serpent's tooth it is to have a thankless child!* I am cut to the quick, as is her intention, and yet I am impressed that she has managed to salvage such elegant verse from the ruins of her mind. Still, I feel like an evil daughter, the bad seed, the *thankless child,* even speculating that death before Parkinson's is finished with her might be a preferable fate.

These are the anguished thoughts that keep adult children awake in the night. I push them aside; I'd rather leave them to philosophers and ethicists to debate. I don't know the answers; I don't know what is best for my mother. I pray for God to hold her close in her suffering, and, like a coward, I pray that somehow, the hard decisions will be made for me.

Mortality/Death

Death's Small Gift

(2009)

My dad died on the Fourth of July. Tired of his losing battle against congestive heart failure and kidney failure, he had decided on July 2 to stop his thrice-weekly dialysis treatments. The hospice people came to the house and set him up with a hospital bed, a sweet and caring nurse, and a prescription for morphine. My five siblings and our families began to gather, believing my dad had a week or so to live. My parents' home was full of kids and noise again.

On the morning of the Fourth, however, only a few of us were in the house when Father Mac, a family friend and priest, appeared at the door. My dad had been in a deep sleep from about midnight the night before. Father Mac had come to give my dad the sacrament of the anointing of the sick and to pray last rites. My sister and her husband, my mom, my youngest daughter, and I were the only ones in the house. At Father Mac's invitation, we formed a circle around my dad's bed and prayed together. Father Mac anointed my dad's forehead and gave him absolution.

My youngest daughter, at 17, had recently followed in the footsteps of her three older siblings and had stopped going to

143

Mass regularly after being confirmed. But participating in the last rites for her grandpa resonated deeply with her. "Isn't it weird, Mom," she said later, "that when Father Mac got here, only the practicing Catholics were in the house?" She meant that the family atheists were not in the other room, making the usual disparaging comments about weak people who needed to lean on the crutch of religion. It seemed that as soon as Father Mac left, the house again filled with people who would not have wanted to join in prayer. We'd been given a holy moment in God's presence.

My dad never regained consciousness. We took turns sitting with him, talking to him, telling him about the kids splashing in the pool and the schedule for fireworks. The hospice nurse had told us that even if he wasn't responsive, he might still hear us. So we talked. He seemed to be resting peacefully, without the groans and grimaces and strange syllables that had punctuated his sleep for the last few months. Around 6:00 p.m., he stopped breathing. He exhaled, and just never inhaled.

On the following Sunday, my daughter said, "I kind of want to go to Mass with you." Just like that. And it occurred to me that, in the midst of crippling sadness and mourning, a small light was shining, enkindling my daughter's gentle conversion of heart. My dad had gone home. Maybe she's thinking of coming home, too.

A Labor of Love and Loss
(2019)

You know that instant alarm you feel when a loved one's normal voice on the phone is not normal? I knew something was wrong by the way my daughter said, "Mom?"

A mother's mind races in a thousand directions at that tone. *What happened?* What happened was indeed tragic, horrible, unbelievable: her friend May had died in childbirth.

In a hospital. In the United States. May had gone in with her husband to have a baby, a routine event, even if it feels amazing to the expectant couple. But something went wrong. Only the father and the baby went home.

She's a baby girl—a tiny, perfect, beautiful, brand-new baby, whose birthday is always going to be the day her mother died. As noted: tragic, horrible, unbelievable.

And I am wondering, questioning, silently: *Where was God in that labor room? Why her? Why a young first-time mother? Why not take an old bird like me? Can I go back in time and volunteer to switch places?*

I know that's not how God works. Not that I know how God does work. Not that anything I think I know about how God works or doesn't work is accurate.

A lump of disbelief, a railing at injustice, and a stunned sadness sit in the hearts of those who knew this bright and vibrant woman. We don't know what to do. We can try to channel our desolation into researching the facts: According to the Centers for Disease Control, each year about 700 women in the United States die from pregnancy or delivery complications. The maternal death rate in the U.S. is higher than in any other developed country. The risk of death is three to four times higher for Black women than for white women. Here we find plenty of outrage, both for the numbers and the racial discrepancy. May is now counted in this ill-fated group of 700: as with any mortality statistic, however, one is too many if you know her. If she is yours.

We can sandwich our sorrow into educated action that might tackle the causes of maternal death, or into advocacy for safer conditions for childbirth, for better access to prenatal care, for wider support for pregnant women and single parents, for something, anything, good to come of tragedy. We can contribute to the GoFundMe account for the young family, or drop off nutritious meals, or offer our time to help get stuff done, or pray, pray, pray, even as we know that whatever we do will not change the past. Whatever we give will not be enough.

We can focus on the kindness of community, seeing how folks far and wide have come together to support this family of two. We can be touched by the way disaster can bring out the best in people, and for the way we are momentarily mindful of the fortune we enjoy, and of the urge to tell our loved ones that we love them. These are small comforts. But they aren't nothing.

May was hugely loved, by her family and friends and co-workers and acquaintances. She is just as hugely mourned. She died on what was supposed to be one of the happiest days of her life. I say one of the happiest because a mother counts the days of each of her children's births as among the happiest. I push down a wave of guilt for the extravagant, unearned blessings of my four children and my decades of bursting-with-love motherhood. May should be here to have more babies. She should be here to nurse and swaddle her daughter, to change diapers and lose sleep and fret and worry and marvel and sing tender songs in the middle of the night and feel overwhelmed by it all and delight in every first thing her little girl does in life. She should be here. We all think it: it's not fair.

It never is.

It's also not easy. It's not easy to hug a new father who is awash in the deepest grief and the loneliest joy of his life. It's not easy to fish around for the good and right words to say, even as we perceive that there aren't any. It's not easy to see a husband without a wife, an infant without a mother. None of it is easy.

But it is rich, this life we are given, rich in complexity and sorrow and gladness and challenge and change. It is rich in unexpected turns and unbidden burdens and sudden, astonishing grace. We don't anticipate young mothers dying at a moment devoted to birth, and yet we know it happens. We know about death—we have experienced its very real, cavernous loss—and yet we are caught unawares by it. We count on life—we take for granted another morning, another cup of coffee, another chance to make love—and yet these terrible things that happen slap us awake with the reminder of the ephemeral nature of us on this earth. We can all disappear just like that.

I imagine May living on in her child, in the way her daughter might one day tuck her hair behind her ear or laugh at a lame Dad-joke. May is gone, but her DNA remains. Her gift to posterity remains. Her powerful love remains. I like to think her spirit remains. I like to think of the fierce unseen presence of a mother watching over her daughter. I like to think of God mingling among us, sad with us, holding us up, loving us, even if we do not comprehend or agree with God's will. I don't know if anything I am thinking is true. But I'm thinking it anyway.

Shopping with the Dead

(2018)

One of my sisters and I have embraced a tradition that may seem morbid to some: we take the day of the anniversary of each of our parents' death off and spend it together. We go to the cemetery and to Mass and gather the memories and the mourning into our arms and hearts for one more year. Since our dad died on the Fourth of July, a national holiday, getting together is easy. If you knew my dad, with his hearty, charming, larger-than-life presence, you'd understand how appropriate this anniversary is. But our mother died on the first of March, an unassuming, trickier day to get together, and if you knew my mother, with her darker, insecure, behind-the-scenes chafing in the shadow of her spouse's spotlight, you'd understand the aptness of this day. Nevertheless, and with a side serving of guilt for being few in number, my sister and I made certain to meet on this past March 1.

Our pious plans for the day, however, went awry. We did buy flowers and go to the cemetery and clean up our parents' gravesites and reminisce and say a prayer, but our lunch date with a good friend—our beloved Father Mac, who buried our parents and has presided over many other sacraments for our family members—fell through at the last minute. As we floated ideas about how to spend our afternoon together, I confessed to my sister, a bit tentatively, feeling sacrilegious, that I intended to stop by Nordstrom's before I drove home later that day.

My sister's face brightened. We realized at the same moment that going to the mall was exactly the right way to honor our dead mother, a shopping warrior.

Sometimes, when a loved one is ill for a long time before dying, we forget what that person was like in healthier times. Our mother had been stricken with Parkinson's disease and with dementia, and her last few years were not easy, for her or for us. Mind you, my mother was never a particularly positive person, but as she deteriorated physically and mentally, she became more negative, more accusatory, more unhappy about everything, and just plain meaner. (I feel mean-spirited myself writing these things now that she's gone, but I'm going for honesty here.) My mother was a difficult person to love, but we did our best to love her until the end. And many years ago, when she was mobile and lucid, one of my mother's favorite activities was to go shopping with her four daughters.

In some ways, buying us stuff was how my mother showed love. Any upcoming event was all the excuse needed to go clothes shopping. Because my mother felt she was overweight, she rarely bought outfits for herself on these marathon trips: she bought her clothes through mail-order catalogues, pre-internet mail-ordering being another of her passions. But she loved dressing up her slimmer daughters. These day-long excursions entailed us piling into the biggest dressing room we could find, as long as it had a bench for our mother, and trying on things that we ourselves could never have afforded, and our mother signaling yea or nay. "Just don't tell your father what we spent," she'd say conspiratorially, and we all promised secrecy, even though it didn't really matter if he found out. It was a game they played with money. Our shopping trips included a lunch break, usually at a fancier place than any of us would have chosen, and again at my mother's expense. This was her idea of fun.

As a young mother on a tight budget, I used to wonder how my mother derived such joy from buying extravagant things for her daughters. Now that I am an older mother with a better cash flow and adult children with their own economic struggles, I totally get it. Maybe because I remember those days of dizzying gratitude and the feeling of leaving the real world behind for a brief respite while shopping with my mother and sisters, I now delight in treating my kids whenever I can.

My mother was neither a saint nor a heroine, but she loved us in her way. She had grown up desperately poor and never really sated her need for security. She often resented my father's easy way with people but was afraid to risk rejection on her own. She hid behind her husband and fretted and fumed. When my dad died, it was as though she needed someone else to be mad at, so each of us spent some time in her glare. But as my sister and I went to Nordstrom's—I bought criminally expensive anti-wrinkle cream and she a stunning purple dress for a charity event—we felt our mother's presence on the bench in the dressing room. Later, at lunch, we felt strangely at peace with our conflicted and complicated feelings about our mother. We hadn't shopped with her in many years, but her long-ago, carefree spirit revisited us that day. Her laugh and her quick wit and her generosity came back to us. We had perhaps honored her memory more fittingly than we had on past anniversaries. It was odd for two grown women to get teary-eyed in a department store dressing room, but I guess that's where we mourned our mother this year. Shopping was our prayer, an unlikely walk with God into Nordstrom's.

Postscript

Back when this book was in its infancy, I explained the title to my youngest daughter, describing my guiding premise about every hill of beans being proportional to our seemingly unremarkable lives and so on. "Oh," she said, "you mean first-world problems."

Well, no, not what I meant, as the balloon of my ambition deflated. I grant that my lived experience with problems is first-world, but my hope is that we can gain insight from, or at least commiserate over, the examining and sharing of issues that are huge only to us. The word "compassion," after all, literally means "suffering together." Our feelings of sadness or anger or frustration are valid and real, no matter the size of our troubles, no matter how small they may shrink when compared to our blessings.

But what do I mean? Since this daughter was the one who excoriated the non-happy ending of the movie we made her watch, it seems appropriate to make a final nod to *Casablanca*. Rick denies being noble, but his self-sacrifice is the essence of nobility as he trades away his happiness for the greater good of the Resistance. He does the right thing, and he pays for it. On his hill of beans, the antihero transforms into unsung hero. His story is a template for our stories, a tale of imperfection suffused with grace.

Every hill of beans we encounter on the journey is a chance for us to navigate the best course around it or over it or through it, to face each earthly obstacle, to rise above the many challenges of a unique but ordinary life. With God's help, with grace, with luck, with humor, we may find that we are the saints of the everyday.

Also by Valerie Schultz:

Overdue
A Dewey Decimal System of Grace
By Valerie Schultz

Paperback, 184 pp.
$19.95
eBook $16.99

"*Overdue* is a rare, sometimes raw, view of human dignity through the eyes and heart of a prison librarian. Valerie Schultz writes with great insight and compassion, without apology or preaching. *Overdue* is a short course in caring."
   —Mary Margaret (Sr. Meg) Funk, OSB, author of, *Renouncing Violence: Practice from the Monastic Tradition.*

For more books from *Give Us This Day* and to place an order, visit GUTD.net/Books or call 800-858-5450.

Give Us This Day is a personal daily prayer book published monthly by Liturgical Press.

For more information or to request a sample copy of *Give Us This Day*, visit GUTD.net or call 888-259-8470.